Fascinating Cities

By
Cynthia Adams

Cover Design by
Annette Hollister-Papp

Cover Illustrations by
Julie Anderson

Inside Illustrations by
Marc F. Johnson

Publishers
Instructional Fair • TS Denison
Grand Rapids, Michigan 49544

Credits

Author: Cynthia G. Adams
Cover Illustrations: Julie Anderson
Cover Art Direction: Annette Hollister-Papp
Poster Art Direction: Matthew Van Zomeren
Inside Illustrations: Marc F. Johnson
Project Director: Danielle de Gregory
Editors: Lynita Strei, Danielle de Gregory
Graphic Layout: Patrice Glendenning,
    Deborah Hanson McNiff

About the Author

Cynthia G. Adams, M.Ed., is a graduate of the University of Cincinnati and Xavier University in Cincinnati, Ohio. She has taught elementary music and special education in Cincinnati public schools for 25 years. In addition, Cynthia G. Adams has been a presenter at local thematic teaching seminars.

Standard Book Number: 1-56822-871-6
Fascinating Cities
Cover and Poster Photographs © Corel Corporation
Copyright © 1999 by Instructional Fair • TS Denison
a division of Tribune Education
2400 Turner Avenue NW
Grand Rapids, Michigan 49544

All Rights Reserved • Printed in the USA

Introduction

Fascinating Cities is a perfect compliment for your units of study on the continents! *Fascinating Cities* provides enough information and activity suggestions for students to learn how to make connections to the real world, past and present, as well as encouraging them to delve into independent research. You can use the materials in *Fascinating Cities* to visit these intriguing places and discover history, art, architecture, math, science, and social studies. Set up your social studies learning center by displaying the four colorful posters that feature beautiful photographs. The reproducible information sheets, web site addresses, and activities pages in *Fascinating Cities* make the creation of your social studies learning center a quick, no-fuss task.

Divided into four continental regions, *Fascinating Cities* includes a description of each continental area before launching the student into an exploration of a landmark and local points of interest. In the back of the book you will find four beautiful posters. These one-sided color posters can easily be pulled out and displayed to show your students images of some of the cities and people.

This resource is intended to help you give your students an understanding of the amazing variety of places throughout our world. Fifty-five specific cities are described and explored. You can introduce your students to a particular place with the reproducible information page. Not only do these information pages give interesting and important information about the cities, they also treat each place as a starting point to learn about cultures, geography, science, art, architecture, and a wealth of other subjects. Each of the information pages contains a few questions, some of which may be answered by carefully reading the page, others require further research in order to challenge your students. Vocabulary words are printed in boldface type to alert you and your students to an avenue of language arts that might need to be researched.

In addition, for each city, the author of *Fascinating Cities* has provided a web site address to further explore and to encourage computer and "web surfing" skills. Note: Because of the mutable nature of the Internet, web sites do change. The sites listed in this resource were current at the time of publication.

Following the information page for each city is a reproducible page with four activities, ready to be cut out and attached to index cards for easy filing in a learning center. These projects can be approached individually or as a team effort. Each of the four activities indicates for which curriculum area it is most appropriate.

To complete your social studies learning center on a particular city, a third reproducible activity page offers a variety of activities—research projects, mazes, crossword puzzles, word searches, or creative writing and drawing exercises.

At the end of *Fascinating Cities*, a quick reference list of *National Geographic* resources with photographic examples of some of the places is provided. If the reference includes any photographs that might cause "undue attention" from students, a note regarding the content of the pictures is included next to the reference.

The *Circling the World* series was developed to encourage students to approach learning using their natural curiosity. An interesting subject naturally invites questions that explore links to other areas and subjects. Discussions about people and places, experiments that spring from a fascinating building material or era, and visual images—all ensure that students remain fascinated by the world and excited to explore a myriad of learning possibilities.

Table of Contents

Africa

Africa...6
Abidjan, Côte d'Ivoire.................................7
   Center Projects 8
   Coffee and Chocolate Products.............9
Addis Ababa, Ethiopia.............................10
   Center Projects 11
   Crossword Puzzle 12
Cairo, Egypt..13
   Center Projects 14
   Vacation Plan 15
Capetown, South Africa............................16
   Center Projects 17
   Apartheid 18
Dakar, Sénégal 19
   Center Projects 20
   Dakar, Sénégal......................................21
Dar es Salaam, Tanzania..........................22
   Center Projects 23
   Dar es Salaam, Tanzania 24
Lagos, Nigeria...25
   Center Projects 26
   Word Search Puzzle 27
Nairobi, Kenya 28
   Center Projects 29
   Nairobi National Park............................30
Tangier, Morocco 31
   Center Projects 32
   Word Search Puzzle 33

Asia and Australia

Asia and Australia 34
Bangkok, Thailand 35
   Center Projects 36
   Bangkok Atlas..37
Beijing, China 38
   Center Projects 39
   Giant Pandas 40
Calcutta, India..41
   Center Projects 42
   Mother Teresa 43
Damascus, Syria 44
   Center Projects 45
   The Ghutah Oasis 46
Hanoi, Vietnam 47
   Project Center 48
   The One Pillar Pagoda 49

Hong Kong, China.....................................50
   Center Projects 51
   Hong Kong, China..................................52
Isfahan, Iran 53
   Center Projects 54
   Isfahan, Iran 55
Jakarta, Indonesia 56
   Center Projects 57
   Wayang Kulit (Shadow Puppetry) 58
Jerusalem, Israel 59
   Center Projects 60
   Word Search Puzzle 61
Kuala Lumpur, Malaysia 62
   Center Projects 63
   Malaysian Industries 64
Mumbai (Bombay), India...........................65
   Center Projects 66
   Suez Canal 67
Seoul, Korea 68
   Center Projects 69
   Crossword Puzzle 70
Shanghai, China 71
   Center Projects 72
   Shanghai's Future 73
Singapore, Singapore 74
   Center Projects 75
   Land Reclamation 76
Sydney, Australia 77
   Center Projects 78
   Word Search Puzzle 79
Tokyo, Japan...80
   Center Projects 81
   Tokyo, Japan..82

Europe

Europe 83
Amsterdam, Netherlands...........................84
   Center Projects 85
   Anne Frank House 86
Athens, Greece 87
   Center Projects 88
   Crossword Puzzle 89
Barcelona, Spain 90
   Center Projects 91
   Barcelona, Spain 92
Berlin, Germany 93
   Center Projects 94
   Berlin Wall 95

Table of Contents

Budapest, Hungry.................................96
   Center Projects 97
   Word Search Puzzle 98
Edinburgh, Scotland.........................99
   Center Projects 100
   Edinburgh, Scotland....................101
Istanbul, Turkey..............................102
   Center Projects 103
   Istanbul, Turkey 104
Kiev, Ukraine..................................105
   Center Projects 106
   Chernobyl....................................107
London, England.............................108
   Center Projects 109
   Westminster Abbey 110
Madrid, Spain..................................111
   Center Projects 112
   Madrid, Spain..............................113
Moscow, Russia...............................114
   Center Projects 115
   Bolshoi Theater Ballet.................116
St. Petersburg, Russia.....................117
   Center Projects 118
   Peter the Great 119
Paris, France...................................120
   Center Projects 121
   The Musée du Louvre 122
Prague, Czech Republic...................123
   Center Projects 124
   Prague, Czech Republic 125
Rome, Italy.....................................126
   Center Projects 127
   Ancient Rome 128
Stockholm, Sweden.........................129
   Center Projects 130
   Word Search Puzzle 131
Venice, Italy...................................132
   Center Projects 133
   Daily Life in a Canal City.............134
Vienna, Austria...............................135
   Center Projects 136
   Vienna, Austria............................137

North and South America

North and South America..........................138
Bogota, Columbia 139
   Center Projects 140
   Bogota, Columbia........................141
Buenos Aires, Argentina................142
   Center Projects 143
   Buenos Aires, Argentina..............144
Havana, Cuba.................................145
   Center Projects 146
   Havana, Cuba...............................147
La Paz, Bolivia...............................148
   Center Projects 149
   La Paz, Bolivia.............................150
Mexico City, Mexico 151
   Center Projects 152
   Mexico City, Mexico 153
Montreal, Canada...........................154
   Center Projects 155
   Underground City 156
New York City, United States 157
   Center Projects 158
   Empire State Building 159
Panama City, Panama 160
   Center Projects 161
   Word Search Puzzle......................162
Reykjavik, Iceland..........................163
   Center Projects 164
   Reykjavik, Iceland........................165
Rio de Janeiro, Brazil 166
   Center Projects 167
   Rio de Janeiro, Brazil 168
San Francisco, United States.........169
   Center Projects 170
   Chinatown, San Francisco 171
Toronto, Canada 172
   Center Projects 173
   Toronto, Canada 174
Answer Key 175–176
Reference List............................176

Africa

Africa is the second largest continent. It has 53 independent countries and several political units. It is a continent of contrast, with untouched natural beauty and modern cities, rain forests and deserts.

In the early 1900s, Europeans colonized Africa in order to control its valuable resources. Africans fought the European takeover and by the middle of the century many of the colonies were independent. Unfortunately, many leaders of the new nations were not prepared for the economic and social problems that followed. In some cases, military officers overthrew the new governments and created dictatorships. Wars among culture groups still threaten the continent.

The six countries of northern Africa have close ties to Europe and the Middle East. They form a region apart from the African countries south of the Sahara. Most of the people living in Mauritania, Morocco, Algeria, Tunisia, Libya, and Egypt speak Arabic and practice the Islamic religion.

There are about 731 million people in Africa today. Most of the people live in rural areas, earning money by growing crops or raising livestock. Others have moved to the cities for better jobs and a modern way of life. Many African countries need foreign aid to support their people.

Africa produces most of the world's supply of cassava, cocoa beans, and yams. There are also large deposits of copper, diamonds, gold, and petroleum. Tourists, drawn to the continent because of its wildlife, are important to the economy of Africa. Wildlife, including giraffes, elephants, lions, and zebras, live on the grasslands of eastern and southern Africa.

The continent has the world's longest river, the Nile, the largest desert, the Sahara, and the highest single mountain, Mount Kilimanjaro.

Abidjan, Côte d'Ivoire

Abidjan, which lies along the Ébrié Lagoon, is one of West Africa's most beautiful and busiest port cities. This is a modern city, sometimes called the "Paris of Africa" because of its European-style shops, **condominiums**, and restaurants. It is in **sharp contrast** to the Ivory Coast's small villages where just miles outside the city you are more likely to find straw-roofed huts and mud roads.

The city has five main **districts**: the Plateau, Cocody, Macory, Treichville, and Adjame. The Plateau is the center of Abidjan's business district with high-rise office buildings, French restaurants, and **boutiques**. The Cocody and Macory districts are home to wealthy residents of the city. Their homes have air conditioning, beautiful gardens, and swimming pools. The Macory district has foreign **embassies**, government buildings, and fancy hotels. Also in Macory is the **futuristic** St. Paul's Cathedral. The building looks like an **ivory-tusked** elephant.

Treichville and Adjame are overcrowded with Ivorians and immigrants from other West African countries. Treichville has a large open-air market and street vendors which are famous for a wide **variety** of **exotic** foods and traditional crafts. Some stands feature good luck **charms** called *gris-gris,* which are made from wild animal fur, **hides**, and teeth. At night, the **cobblestone** streets are filled with the sound of traditional African music and dancers.

In the Adjame District, the shores of the Banco River are **lined** with washermen doing the laundry of the wealthier residents of Abidjan. They beat the clothes against the rocks to clean them. Although they never number or mark the clothes, the washermen rarely mix up an **order**.

Answer in complete sentences:

1. What animal does Abidjan's St. Paul's Cathedral resemble?
2. What is gris-gris?
3. Name the five districts of Abidjan.
4. In what part of Africa is the Ivory Coast?
5. Where is the Banco River?

Web Site:

http://www.un.org/Pubs/CyberSchoolBus/special/habitat/profiles/abidjan.shtml

Research

You will need:

✔ nonfiction books about Côte d'Ivoire
✔ paper
✔ pencil

Who was Félix Houphouët-Boigny? What part did he play in Côte d'Ivoire's independence?

Research

You will need:

✔ nonfiction books about Côte d'Ivoire
✔ paper
✔ pencil

What is a *pagne?* Explain how it is worn by both men and women.

Social Studies

You will need:

✔ nonfiction information about French history and the Ivory Coast
✔ paper
✔ pencil

Explain how the people of the Ivory Coast resisted French rule. Make a time line to explain the sequence of events that led to the colony's independence from France.

Music

You will need:

✔ nonfiction books about African musical instruments and Côte d'Ivoire
✔ paper
✔ pencil

What is a *balafon?* Make a drawing of the instrument and explain how it is constructed and played. Choose another African instrument and explain how it is constructed and played.

Coffee and Chocolate Products

Much of the Côte d'Ivoire's coffee beans and cocoa seeds move through the port of Abidjan. These crops are very important to the economy of the country.

Complete two of the following projects on either cocoa or coffee. Use at least three different sources from the library or the Internet to complete each project.

▲ Explain the climate and soil requirements of these crops.

▲ Research the appearance and size of each kind of plant. Make drawings to scale using authentic colors.

▲ Draw a flow chart showing either of the raw products from harvest to the grocery shelf.

▲ Explain the nutritional value or health concerns associated with these products.

▲ Make lists of processed foods that contain either coffee or cocoa. Put a check mark by the products used by your family.

▲ Do research to find how the cocoa and coffee crops were affected by the drought of 1982 to 1984.

Write the name, author, and publisher of your printed sources or the name and web site address of your Internet sources.

Project I

_____

_____

_____

Project II

_____

_____

_____

Addis Ababa, Ethiopia

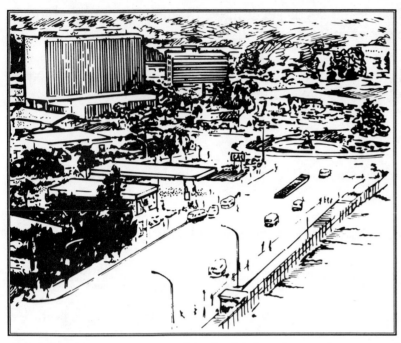

Addis Ababa is located in the center of Ethiopia on the **slopes** of the Entoto Mountains. Early in the 1900s, Addis Ababa had **shortages** of wood for **fuel** and building materials. **Eucalyptus** trees were brought in from Australia and planted in every empty space in the city. This saved the city from being **abandoned**. Today, most of the buildings in Addis Ababa are made of eucalyptus wood.

One of Africa's largest and most famous open-air markets, the *Mercato*, is located in the old central section of the city. Today, the *Mercato* serves as a kind of inland port for central Ethiopia. People from all over the country go there to buy and sell anything from vegetables, grains, and animals, to gold and silver jewelry. This **bustling hub** of activity is also a favorite spot for **pickpockets**. This can be a problem in many large cities.

Housing in Addis Ababa ranges from modern high-rise apartment buildings to African-style mud huts. Many years ago, the nobles of Emperor Menelik II were given land on the hilltops of Addis Ababa. Their servants built neighborhoods called *safars* on the nearby hillsides. Poverty is most common around the central business section of the city.

The traditional food of Ethiopia is becoming very popular around the world. *Injera* is a bread with the **texture** of foam rubber. It is made from **millet** flour and yeast that is left to go sour for three days. Then, it is cooked on a clay board. *Injera* is served with different kinds of *wat*, which is a fiery hot sauce. *Wat* can be made with chicken, beans, beef, fish, lamb, or vegetables.

Answer in complete sentences:

1. In what part of Ethiopia is Addis Ababa?
2. What was done to solve a wood shortage in the 1900s?
3. What is the Mercato?
4. What is a safar?
5. Name a problem that is common in large cities.

Web Site:

http://www.macalester.edu/~kshively/intro.html

Language Arts

You will need:

✓ nonfiction information about Ethiopia

✓ paper

✓ pencil

Explain daily life for a typical child in Ethiopia. Describe her or his home. Does the child attend school? What is the major religion? What are popular foods? Draw a child in native dress.

Science

You will need:

✓ nonfiction information (field book) about trees

✓ paper

✓ pencil

Many eucalyptus trees grow in and near Addis Ababa. What conditions are best for growing this species? What products does the eucalyptus tree provide? Make a drawing of the eucalyptus leaf.

Geography

You will need:

✓ encyclopedia volume E

✓ white drawing paper

✓ colored pencils

Draw a map of Ethiopia. For each city, include an icon that explains the main products or attractions. Show these places: Addis Ababa, Djibouti, Akaki (a center for light industries including textiles and food processing), Nazareth (a sugar processing center), and Lake Bishofu, a lake area popular for vacations.

Social Studies

Compare and contrast two neighborhoods—a *safar* and a wealthier one. Would you have enough food to eat? Would you have toys with which to play? Would your home have running water? What would your day be like?

Addis Ababa, Ethiopia

Crossword Puzzle

ACROSS

1. People who cause a problem in many large cities
6. Kind of flour used to make *injera*
8. Foam rubber-type bread
12. Addis Ababa is located on the slopes of the ___.
13. Traditional African home
15. African city that suffered a wood shortage in the 1900s

DOWN

2. Trees brought to Addis Ababa from Australia
3. People who were given land by Emperor Menelik II
4. Kind of poultry with which *wat* might be made
5. What *Injera* is cooked on
7. Length of time *injera* dough is left to go sour
9. Hillside neighborhoods in Addis Ababa
10. Where pickpockets work
11. Country in which Addis Ababa is located

Cairo, Egypt

The Nile is the world's longest river. It flows directly through Cairo, Egypt's capital. The waters of the Nile give **relief** from the hot, dry air that blows from the surrounding deserts. The city only gets about 1 inch (2.54 cm) of rainfall all year long.

Cairo is an ancient city where history has become a part of modern everyday life. The pyramids of Giza, built about 4,500 years ago, can be seen from the windows of most Cairo office towers. Restaurants, coffeeshops, and markets are housed in 1,000-year-old stone buildings. In the Northern Cemetery, the living and the dead **exist** side by side, as homeless people have made temporary homes out of the **tombs**. Thousands of people inhabit the cemetery, popularly called the City of the Dead.

The oldest section of the city is called Islamic Cairo and has changed little in centuries, except for the addition of cars and radios. On the dusty, crowded streets, Toyota sedans and donkeys pulling wooden carts compete for space. This part of Cairo has narrow, winding streets, one of the Middle East's largest street **bazaars**, and at least 300 mosques.

Mosques are the houses of worship for the Islamic religion, which is the most **predominant** religion of Egypt. Islamic officials, called *muezzins*, call Muslims to prayer five times each day from atop the **minarets** of Cairo's mosques. When called to prayer, Muslims must stop what they are doing and pray while facing east. The ceremony of prayer involves washing their faces, hands, and feet. While praying, Muslims sometimes bow or kneel on the ground with their faces on the ground. The noontime prayer every Friday must be **conducted** at a mosque.

The modern sections of Cairo are on the west bank of the Nile and on the islands of Gezira and Roda. These areas have parks, hotels, restaurants, and government centers. Middle- and upper-class citizens live in this section of the city in condominiums or high-rise apartments.

Answer in complete sentences:
1. Describe life in the old section of Cairo.
2. Describe life in the new section of Cairo.
3. What is the City of the Dead?
4. What is the major religion practiced in Cairo?
5. Where are the Great Pyramids?

Web Site:
http://egyptcenter.com/
http://www.coptic.net/Egypt/Cairo/

Research

You will need:

- ✔ encyclopedia volumes A and N
- ✔ paper
- ✔ pencil

Research the history and construction of the Aswan High Dam and Lake Nasser. How has the dam influenced agriculture in the area?

Social Studies

You will need:

- ✔ international cookbook and nonfiction books on Egypt
- ✔ paper
- ✔ pencil

What is *ful?* What are the main ingredients and how is the dish traditionally eaten? Make a cookbook with three of these recipes: *hummus, kebabs, babaganoush, aysh,* or *ful.* If possible, prepare a snack of *hummus* and pita bread to share with the class.

Language Arts

You will need:

- ✔ paper
- ✔ pencil

Cairo has a severe housing shortage. There is even a "City of the Dead" built by people living in one of the city's cemeteries. Describe what it would be like if you and your family lived in a cemetery.

Social Studies

You will need:

- ✔ nonfiction information about Islam and Egypt
- ✔ paper
- ✔ pencil

Explain the styles of dress worn by Muslim women, the *niqab* and the *hijab.* Make drawings to show the differences. Describe traditional clothing for Egyptian men, the *galabiyya.*

Vacation Plan

Do research to plan a trip to Egypt. Set a budget amount and then start planning. Find out what an itinerary is and then make one.

▲ Telephone airlines to find out fares, schedules, and lengths of the flights.

▲ Use the Internet, the travel section of the library, or a travel agency to find out about hotels or hostels.

▲ What kinds of foods can you eat in restaurants and how much money will you need for meals? Do not forget about snacks. Will you need to purchase water?

▲ Are there any shots you should get before leaving home? How far in advance will you need to plan any immunizations?

▲ Can you bring your pet along? Is there a quarantine for animals?

▲ Plan a phone call home during your vacation. What is the time difference?

▲ What is the current exchange rate?

▲ How much cash should you exchange before leaving?

▲ Whom do you tip? Hotel maids? Cab drivers? Bathroom attendants?

▲ What kinds of clothing will you need?

▲ Will your hair dryer work in Egypt? Why or why not?

Capetown, South Africa

Capetown, South Africa, is one of the most scenic cities in Africa, surrounded by mountains and overlooking the Atlantic Ocean. It is easy to see why the area, first called Cape of Good Hope, was colonized so quickly by Europeans passing by in search of a sea route to the East. White, sandy beaches, **vineyards**, and wildlife reserves are within minutes from Capetown, making it a popular tourist attraction.

Table Mountain is a national landmark which can be seen **towering** above Capetown. A **cable car,** taking visitors to the flat top of the mountain, travels through an area of incredible natural beauty that is part of the Cape Floral Kingdom. Unusual varieties of birds and butterflies can be seen on the mountain. The Cape Peninsula is one of the richest plant regions in the world, with an **estimated** 2,200 different species of plants.

The Cape area was colonized by the English and the Dutch in the 17th century. The two countries shared control of South Africa until 1948 when the Afrikaner National Party gained a political **majority**. The Europeans of South Africa created the policy of **apartheid** to **assure** their continued economic and social control. Not until 1991 were the laws of apartheid finally **abolished**. Nelson Mandela was elected in 1994 as the first democratic president of South Africa.

Robben Island, which is sort of the Alcatraz of South Africa, is off the coast of Capetown. It was the prison that held famous black leaders and **revolutionaries** during apartheid, including Nelson Mandela. The prison does not hold criminals any longer, but is open for public tours. When Robben Island was first opened to the public, visitors would line up at 4:00 a.m., to be among the 300 people allowed per day to visit the **former** prison.

Answer in complete sentences:

1. Name two European countries that colonized South Africa.
2. Why were apartheid laws created?
3. What would you see on a hike up Table Mountain?
4. Where was Nelson Mandela imprisoned?
5. When was apartheid enacted? When was it abolished?

Web Sites:

http://www.city.net/countries/south_africa/cape_town
http://www.ctcc.gov.za/

Science

You will need:

➤ travel brochures on Capetown
➤ nonfiction books about exotic bird species
➤ paper
➤ pencil
➤ colored pencils

Design a travel brochure for Table Mountain, including statistics, cable car information, and details about the flora and fauna. Explain the characteristics and habits of Capetown's sunbirds and sugarbirds.

Language Arts

You will need:

➤ biography of Nelson Mandela
➤ paper
➤ pencil

List 10 events from the life of Nelson Mandela. Explain his activities with the African National Congress. What is Nelson Mandela doing today?

Social Studies

You will need:

➤ encyclopedia volumes S and C
➤ world atlas
➤ paper
➤ pencil

South Africa is unusual because it has three capitals. Explain the activities that take place in each one. Locate the cities on a map and estimate the distances among them.

Social Studies

You will need:

➤ nonfiction books on diamond mines, diamonds, and South Africa
➤ paper
➤ pencil

What are the working conditions in a diamond mine? What are workers in South Africa's diamond mines paid? How much do diamonds sell for in a jewelry store?

Apartheid

Use a reference book or an encyclopedia to answer these questions about apartheid in South Africa.

1. What does apartheid mean in the Africaans language?

   _____

2. What were the three classifications of race under apartheid?

   _____, _____, _____

3. How did the African National Congress oppose apartheid?

   _____

   _____

   _____

4. What forced the South African government to repeal apartheid laws?

   _____

   _____

5. What is the current policy of discrimination and segregation for nonwhites and whites in South Africa, today?

   _____

   _____

6. What were some of the countries in the world that opposed apartheid?

   _____

   _____

7. How did other countries try to influence South Africa to end apartheid?

   _____

   _____

   _____

   _____

Dakar, Sénégal

Dakar is the westernmost city on the **mainland** of Africa. Its location makes it a perfect trading port because the peninsula sticks way out into the Atlantic Ocean and turns southward, protecting the harbor from bad weather. Dakar was colonized by France in 1857. French is still the official language, even though Sénégal became an independent nation in 1960. However the African language *Wolof* is spoken more often than French.

The port at Dakar is large enough to hold several ships. The port has refrigerated **warehouses** and **pipelines** to handle many kinds of **cargo**. It has **prospered** as an important **commercial** shipping center. It is one of the best **equipped** shipping docks in West Africa.

Dakar is a beautiful combination of traditional African richness and reminders of the French colonial days. Dakar's wide avenues are lined with tall, modern office buildings, French restaurants, and apartments. It is a city where businesspeople and tourists, Western clothes and African dress, colonial-style villas and huge, modern buildings, big supermarkets and small boutiques can all exist side by side.

The Medina section, which is the old town, has narrow, winding streets, old buildings, and no electricity or **sewage** system. It is not a poor section of Dakar; it is just old-fashioned. 20 is home to many West African immigrants and native Senagalese alike. Medina features a traditional street market selling foods, spices, flowers, and handmade fabrics and baskets. The market women display fresh flowers by wearing them as brilliant **headdresses**.

Answer in complete sentences:

1. What European country colonized Sénégal?
2. When did Sénégal gain its independence?
3. Where is Dakar located on the African continent?
4. What shipping activities are possible at Dakar's seaport?
5. What can a visitor see in the Medina section of Dakar?

Web Site:
http://www.earth2000.com/senegal/

Science

You will need:

✔ nonfiction information about Sénégal
✔ paper
✔ pencil

Peanuts and sorghum are the main crops of Sénégal. Explain how each of them is grown and how they are prepared as food. Bring samples of each to share with the class.

Language Arts

You will need:

✔ paper
✔ pencil

Why do people move from the rural areas into the cities? Discuss life in the cities and rural regions of Sénégal.

Social Studies

You will need:

✔ nonfiction information on Sénégal
✔ paper
✔ pencil

What kinds of activities go on at the Dakar seaport? What are some of the places that cargo goes to when it leaves Dakar?

Language Arts

You will need:

✔ book of African legends

Read several of the stories. Learn to retell one in the style of a *griot*, a traditional Senegalese storyteller. Demonstrate to your classmates.

Dakar, Sénégal

Research and draw three kinds of boats that can be found at the seaport of Dakar.

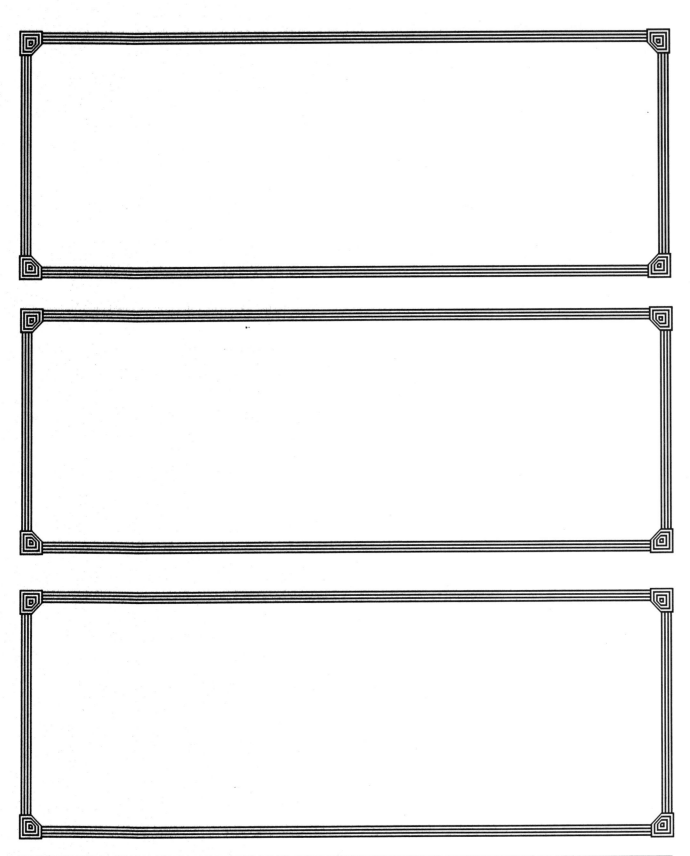

Dar es Salaam, Tanzania

Dar es Salaam is the capital city on the east coast of Tanzania. When the sultan of Zanzibar landed there in 1862, he fell in love with the peace and **tranquility** and wanted it to be the spot for his grand palace. It was to be Zanzibar's new capital. The sultan gave it the name *Dar es Salaam,* which in Swahili means "haven of peace." He was never able to build his palace, due to his death. However, the city grew and expanded without the sultan's help.

Dar es Salaam was a simple fishing village when the sultan first arrived. Even though Dar es Salaam has grown into a **thriving** commercial center, the past is still **visible**. Alongside the modern ocean-going **vessels** are small wooden sailboats called *dhows* that the Tanzanians use to carry people and **goods** from port to port. The **whitewashed** stone buildings with red tiled roofs along the coast and the graceful dhows make Dar es Salaam a **timeless** setting.

Dar es Salaam is the perfect spot to rest and buy supplies before heading out on an African **safari**. Tanzania is famous for the guided tours through game reserves where animals are free to **roam** and are protected from hunters. You can catch a glimpse of elephants, lions, leopards, giraffes, and other wild animals in their natural **habitat**.

Although Dar es Salaam is a modern city with high-rise office towers and government centers, there is a colorful mix of tradition with modern fashion. Women commonly wear Western-style clothing, but with an added sense of **culture**. Long pieces of brightly-colored and boldly-printed fabric, called *khangas,* are worn over other clothes. *Khangas* can be used in many different ways: as headdresses, skirts, or draped over a shoulder. There is usually a theme to the pattern and a wise Swahili saying on the bottom. Men wear something similar, called *kikoi,* tied around their waists.

Answer in complete sentences:

1. Who founded Dar es Salaam in 1862?
2. What is the meaning of the Swahili name *Dar es Salaam?*
3. Where is Zanzibar?
4. What is a dhow?
5. What is the purpose of a game reserve?

Web Site:

http://www.tiac.net/users/dmcooper/rainbow.html

Research

You will need:
- ✔ nonfiction information about Tanzania
- ✔ paper
- ✔ pencil

Who is Julius Kambarage Nyerere? Explain his plan for society called *ujamaa*. Was it successful?

Social Studies/Geography

You will need:
- ✔ nonfiction information about Tanzania
- ✔ map of Tanzania
- ✔ colored pencils
- ✔ paper

Locate Dar es Salaam, Zanzibar, Dodoma, Serengeti National Park, Selous Game Reserve, and Lake Victoria on the map. Create a travel brochure for at least two of these places.

Art

You will need:
- ✔ nonfiction information about international stamps
- ✔ paper
- ✔ markers

Tanzania issues about 300 different stamp designs each year. Select a theme and design at least three stamps. Include the county name and price in Tanzania shillings.

Social Studies

You will need:
- ✔ paper
- ✔ pencil

Make a shopping list and menu of what you would eat if you had no refrigerator. How often would you have to buy groceries?

Dar es Salaam, Tanzania

Many of the vehicles in the streets of Dar es Salaam are human-powered. They may be transporting items like food, clothing, newspapers, or business packages.

Think about life in Tanzania's capital and design a human-powered vehicle that you would like to use. Be sure to include the name of your business and identify what product you are transporting.

Lagos, Nigeria

Lagos is located in southwest Nigeria, the most **populous** state in Africa. The city is on the mainland and four small islands in the Gulf of Guinea. It is a city that grew out of oil riches, but is now overcrowded, polluted, and still in political **chaos**. The suburbs are more **picturesque** and are in great **contrast** to downtown Lagos. The suburbs have well-kept lawns, flowering trees, and old colonial-style houses and buildings.

Lagos was a major slave market until it became a British **protectorate** in 1851 and the British wanted to end the slave trade. The British ran the country **indirectly, appointing** local chiefs. After World Wars I and II, the people of Nigeria wanted independence and in 1963, they got it. Nigeria became a republic and Dr. Nnamdi Azikiwe was its first president. However, the country has never gained a solid, **stable** government and even today, there is unrest.

The high oil prices in the 1970s made Nigeria rich. Thousands of people **flocked** there, looking for work. In the 1980s, oil prices fell and the country's money dried up. Many of the people were unemployed and oil companies went broke. The city has survived because Lagos is Nigeria's chief port and commercial center, handling about 2 million tons of cargo each year. Animal **hides, cacao**, peanuts, and **timber** are shipped through its ports to markets around the world.

Most people in Lagos are of the Yoruba culture group. About half are Muslim. In the city, people live in modern apartments and travel **paved** roads. They work as doctors, lawyers, teachers, or in service or government jobs. Most people choose to dress in Western-style clothing. Visitors can watch artists make wood carvings and **mosaics** at the craft center in the National Museum in Lagos. Batik fabrics, baskets, and jewelry are popular **souvenir** items.

Answer in complete sentences:

1. What product made Nigeria a rich country?
2. How are the suburbs of Lagos different from the inner city?
3. What traditional crafts are popular with tourists?
4. What culture group makes up most of the population of Lagos?
5. Explain the location of Lagos on the African continent.

Web Site:
http://city.net/countries/nigeria/

Language Arts

You will need:

- ✔ nonfiction information about Nigeria
- ✔ paper
- ✔ pencil

Who is Wole Soyinka? Explain his contribution to Nigerian literature. What major award did he win? What humanitarian contributions has he made to society?

Music

You will need:

- ✔ nonfiction information about Nigeria and musical instruments
- ✔ paper
- ✔ pencil
- ✔ art supplies

What are juju bands? What are talking drums? Make drawings of three differently shaped Nigerian drums.

Research/Art

You will need:

- ✔ nonfiction information on batik
- ✔ markers
- ✔ pencil
- ✔ paper

Write a paragraph describing the technique of batik. Then use markers to show examples of designs and what kinds of clothing they are used for.

Art

You will need:

- ✔ nonfiction information on mosaics
- ✔ colored construction paper
- ✔ glue
- ✔ scissors

Cut pieces of construction paper and glue them in a design on another piece of paper. Look at pictures of real mosaics for ideas on how to make your own.

Lagos, Nigeria

Word Search Puzzle

```
W A E E S C I D L L A G O S R M B T
M A H T I A U I P E A N U T S O P E
U R E C S I T F M G O I L T T S Y P
S T S N S I M B A S K E T S U A C O
L N N G U L F O F G U I N E A I C A
I N X C C B P A Y S I L R C D U
M L R A B A T I K N G E Y R E S U O
E R E R H H E R B N T A D T P O R T
R E Y G L O C N I A M I E C A A M N
A T O O H E P V R D S K M T A E E A
H S R B D T R O F S R T N B T C N R
O O U V A A T C D A N S I T E T A B
V O B T C C N G M N A L I T A R A O
G B A D E E F E S R T E R R Z L G N
T Y O T T I V R P O P U L O U S D D
E O O R D A D P X O N N I G E R I A
W R C S L D T E D H C T T A I E M E
P E W S B A E B E T E E E C D E A F
```

Look for these words:

POPULOUS	PROTECTORATE
SLAVE MARKET	OIL
TIMBER	CACAO
PEANUTS	BATIK
MOSAICS	WOOD CARVINGS
LAGOS	NIGERIA
PORT	GULF OF GUINEA
CARGO	MUSLIM
YORUBA	BASKETS

Nairobi, Kenya

Nairobi is an exciting and **cosmopolitan** city in Eastern Africa. It is probably one of the only places in the world where you can see cheetahs, tigers, giraffes, and rhinos wandering free with a city **skyline** in the background. It is a very popular place for **safaris**; the word *kenya* in Swahili means "safari."

Nairobi is a very **appealing** city. Its wide streets are lined with **hibiscus** bushes and **jacaranda** trees which bloom pale purple flowers. Downtown Nairobi has high-rise offices, government buildings, and banks. There are also bookshops, hotels, and restaurants—all the modern **conveniences** you may have missed while travelling across the safari lands of Kenya. Most of Nairobi's people live in apartments outside the city center. The country is populated with over 60 different culture groups of people, making it a varied and interesting place.

The capital is also the country's **academic** and cultural center. The University of Nairobi and Kenyatta University are located in Nairobi. The National Museum has interesting collections about wild animals and **prehistoric** humans. Kenya is the sight where some of the oldest signs of human settlements have been found. It is sometimes called "the cradle of humanity." Also located in Nairobi is Snake Park, which has examples of almost all of East Africa's species of snakes. The snakes can be viewed in glass cages or in open **pits**.

Nairobi National Park is a wildlife sanctuary without bars or cages. Only a few miles outside of the city, the park has all of Africa's big game animals, except for elephants.

Answer in complete sentences:
1. What is the meaning of the Swahili word kenya?
2. How many different culture groups live in Kenya?
3. What wildlife sanctuary is a tourist attraction near Nairobi?
4. Describe downtown Nairobi.
5. Where in Kenya is Nairobi located?

Web Sites:
http://www.rcbowen.com/kenya/cities/nairobi.html
http://travel.yahoo.com/destinations/Africa/Countries/Kenya/Cities/Nairobi/
http://www.city.net/countries/kenya/nairobi/

Social Studies

You will need:
- ✔ paper
- ✔ pencil

Brainstorm a list of jobs in the city of Nairobi that have been created because of tourism.

Research

You will need:
- ✔ nonfiction books about Kenya and Nairobi
- ✔ encyclopedia volumes K and N
- ✔ paper
- ✔ pencil
- ✔ scissors
- ✔ glue stick
- ✔ crayons

Design a flag or coat of arms for the city of Nairobi. Color it and cut it out. Glue it to a sheet of paper. Write a paragraph explaining the importance of each image and color.

Art

You will need:
- ✔ art supplies
- ✔ shoe box

Make a diorama showing one area in the city. You may choose a street scene, Nairobi National Park, or the railroad construction camp.

Language Arts

You will need:
- ✔ tourist brochures showing the Nairobi National Park
- ✔ paper
- ✔ pencil

Pretend you are a tour guide at the Nairobi National Park. Write 10 questions a tourist might ask you. Find the answers to the questions.

Nairobi National Park

This wildlife preserve is located just outside of the city. It is fenced on the Nairobi side but open to the migration of game from the Athi Plains. It is possible to see rhinos, hippos, lions, leopards, giraffes, zebras, cheetahs, warthogs and antelope. The park is open to the public from sunrise to sunset. For safety, visitors are asked to stay inside their cars or buses. Of course, hunting is not allowed.

Directions:
Lead the tour bus through the maze by passing the animals in alphabetical order.

Tangier, Morocco

Tangier lies just 12 miles (19.3 km) from the coast of Spain, directly across the Strait of Gibraltar at the entrance to the Mediterranean Sea. It has long been known as a resort center and tourist's delight with white-sand beaches and mild weather all year long. Morocco's capital is in Rabat, to the west, where the weather can be hot and miserable in the summer. So the country's government business moves to Tangier for two months of the year.

Morocco has been run by many different European countries. Tangier was **declared** an international city from 1923 to 1956. This **status** made Tangier an inviting place for people from all over the world. As an international city, Tangier was governed by a **council** of six Moroccan Jews, six Berber Muslims, and **delegates** from Belgium, France, Spain, England, the Netherlands, Italy, and Portugal. This mix of people and culture gave Tangier an international flavor. Many residents still speak French, Spanish, and Arabic. Most people living in Tangier, today, are Berbers or Arabs.

Most of the people in Tangier are of the Islam faith. The architecture reflects this all over Morocco. The mosques and other structures are usually light-colored **stucco** and feature red, green, and blue tile work in intricate patterns. Wood carvings and detailed stone walls are also commonly found around the city. There are not many high-rise buildings, so the **minarets** of the mosques are seen along the skyline.

In its **heyday**, Tangier became the favorite **retreat** and home for many artists, writers, and **philosophers**. For many foreigners, the city was exotic and mysterious. The spicy Mediterranean food and **belly dancing** in the clubs were very different from the typical vacation spot. This popularity greatly **declined** when the city's international status changed. Tangier is still considered the most cosmopolitan city in Morocco.

Answer in complete sentences:

1. Why is Tangier a convenient tourist destination?
2. Who are the Berbers?
3. Who controlled Tangier when it was an international city?
4. What is Morocco's capital city?
5. Why is the capital moved to Tangier for two months each year?

Web Sites:

http://www.maghreb.net/countries/morocco/cities.html
http://www.arab.net/morocco/morocco_contents.html

Research

You will need:

✔ nonfiction information about Islam
✔ paper
✔ pencil

Explain how the people of Tangier celebrate Ramadan. Where else is it celebrated? Compare it with how other cities covered in this center celebrate Ramadan.

Research

You will need:

✔ nonfiction information about Morocco
✔ paper
✔ pencil

What traditional crafts are sold at the town *souk*? Explain the practice of bartering for bargains.

Language Arts

You will need:

✔ nonfiction information about Morocco and Islam
✔ paper
✔ pencil

Women are treated differently than men in Muslim countries. Explain how women live, dress, and work in Tangier.

Social Studies

You will need:

✔ paper
✔ pencil
✔ crayons
✔ markers

Make a drawing of a *kissaria*. This is the main *souk* of a city, surrounded by walls and heavy gates. Set up a *souk* in your classroom. Bring stuff from home to barter.

Tangier, Morocco

Word Search Puzzle

```
L R A B A T E P S D R M N E C P R E
T E L D I U T R S C A A A E O L R E
B D R P Q N E A E L E C T I S L I O
R E B S H B A S S N H O F A M N S R
P A O E R I T I A I B U E W O V E N
E M S E L S L R D I I N E E P O E H
E E B U I L R O H S S C A E O A P C
E C N T A E Y I S S E I A E L R F M
N T R H T H H D M O G L A E I A E B
K A E I E E M C A Y P E E E T B R W
H A D E X L N O H N S H V D A S M E
T E R M O R O C C O C T E A N T R D
M R I O T T D I E B E I E R G T T O
E N W R I T E R S E U G N R S S C R
R O Y B C X S X U M I Y D G I O E T
T M I N A R E T S S T I L E W O R K
F A E A E E E A N L U X S N O G U A
I T A N G I E R S E N R N H D N S S
```

Look for these words:

MOROCCO
RABAT
BERBERS
ISLAM
TILE WORK
EXOTIC
BELLY DANCING
COSMOPOLITAN
PHILOSOPHERS

TANGIER
COUNCIL
ARABS
MOSQUE
MINARETS
MYSTERIOUS
MEDITERRANEAN
ARTISTS
WRITERS

Asia and Australia

Asia covers about one-third of the world's land area. It is the largest continent in both size and population. There are 49 countries on the continent, including China, the most populous nation in the world. India, another Asian country, has the second largest population. The highest point in Asia is Mount Everest in Nepal. The lowest point is at the Dead Sea in Israel and Jordan.

The cities of Asia are very much like Western cities. They have high-rise apartments and office buildings, airports, theaters, television, shopping centers, and factories. The primary religions in Asia are Hinduism, Islam, and Buddhism.

Australia lies in the South Pacific Ocean and the Indian Ocean. It is the only country that is also a continent. It is called the "land down under" because it lies in the Southern Hemisphere. Most of the people live in the two largest cities on the southeastern coast, Sydney and Melbourne. The rest of the continent is thinly populated.

The first people of Australia were Aborigines, most of whom live in rural areas. The majority of Australia's people came from England and Ireland.

Australia is famous for its unusual wildlife, including kangaroos, platypuses, koala, wombats, and tropical birds.

Bangkok, Thailand

Bangkok is the capital and only modern city in Thailand. The Chao Phraya River runs through the city which is called Krung Thep, or "City of Angels," by the Thai people. Bangkok has high-rise buildings, modern museums, and department stores. In smaller villages, many Thai people still live in the **traditional** way on the river. They build wooden houses that stand on **stilts** in the water. Boats **service** the houses along the way; bus boats, mail boats, and even ice cream boats stop at the houses which can be entered on long, wooden **planks**.

Bangkok still has many of these **canal dwellings,** but most people in this big city now live in concrete apartment buildings. A lot of families in Bangkok have houses with modern kitchens, but the stove is always kept in a separate building outside. The weather is too hot and humid to keep a stove inside the house.

Nearly all of Thailand's people are Buddhist. Buddhists **meditate** and do good deeds which they call *tum bun*. If a Buddhist leaves this world having done more *tum bun* than evil, that person can reach *Nirvana,* which is an unearthly, **ideal** existence. Part of doing good deeds includes building temples for Buddha. The best known temple in Bangkok is the *Wat Phra Kaeo,* or Temple of the Emerald Buddha. The temple houses a small statue of Buddha **positioned** on a high **pedestal.** The Emerald Buddha can only be viewed from outside the door. No photographs may be taken because the statue is considered very sacred.

The Thai word for dinner, *gin kow,* means "eat rice." Rice is eaten at every meal. At the main meal, meat or vegetables are poured over rice. The diners sit on the floor around a low table and each person has his or her own bowl of rice. A large **platter** of meat and vegetables is placed in the middle of the table. The meals are eaten with **chopsticks** or flat-bottomed spoons. A bowl of scented water, usually colored pink or blue, is passed around for each person to drink.

Answer in complete sentences:
1. What river flows through Bangkok?
2. What is the meaning of the Thai name Krung Thep?
3. What is the Wat Phra Kaeo?
4. Name one religious practice of Buddhists.
5. What is eaten at every Thai meal?

Web Sites:
http://www.cs.ait.ac.th/~wutt/wutt.html
http://travel.yahoo.com/Destinations/Asia/Countries/Thailand/Cities/Bangkok/

Research

You will need:
- ✔ encyclopedia volume B
- ✔ paper
- ✔ pencil

What are the main beliefs of Buddhists? Explain how monks live in Buddhist monasteries.

Research

You will need:
- ✔ nonfiction information about Bangkok
- ✔ paper
- ✔ pencil

Describe a typical Thai house. Make a drawing that shows the style of construction.

Social Studies

You will need:
- ✔ nonfiction information on Bangkok
- ✔ tourist brochures about Thailand
- ✔ paper
- ✔ pencil

List five attractions that draw visitors to Bangkok. Design a souvenir or postcard for each one. Find out what the Emerald Buddha looks like and draw him.

Art

You will need:
- ✔ nonfiction books about Thailand
- ✔ art supplies
- ✔ glue stick
- ✔ glitter

Read information about the Loi Krathong festival. Make a drawing of the lanterns on the river. Put a dab of glitter on each "lit" candle. Create a mural by drawing a parade of colorfully decorated elephants and water buffalo.

Bangkok Atlas

You will need an encyclopedia and an atlas to complete this sheet. Fill in the blanks to complete your own atlas page for Bangkok.

Thai name _____   Language _____

Longitude/Latitude _____   Monetary unit _____

Land Area _____   Religion _____

Population _____   Climate _____

Draw a map of Thailand showing Bangkok and the Chao Phraya River.

Draw one landmark found in Thailand.

Beijing, China

Beijing is on the northern plain of the **vast** country of China. The capital of China is an exciting place with much to see. It is filled with temples, palaces, bright colors, and lots and lots of people. There are at least 11 million people in this city. So many people, in fact, that China's government has **enacted** laws to encourage families to have no more than one child per family. Families that have more children suffer tax **penalties** or are not allowed to hold many kinds of government jobs. Although this is an unpopular policy with most Chinese people, it has slowed the growing population rate tremendously.

In 1200, the Mongol ruler Kublai Khan began building a settlement on the spot that is now Beijing. Since then, the city has been led by ruling families called dynasties, the first of which was called the Ming Dynasty. Many of the city's beautiful temples and palaces were built by the ruling dynasties and emperors. The Old City of Beijing is what is called the Forbidden City. The city was truly forbidden from any person entering it, except the emperor, his family, and his thousands of servants. The emperor rarely ever left the Forbidden City to travel among his loyal **subjects**. This was not difficult, considering the Forbidden City has over 800 buildings and 9,000 rooms. Today, the buildings are **restored** and used as museums. It is one of Beijing's most popular tourist attractions.

Among the hundreds of temples, palaces, and other amazing historical structures in Beijing is the White Cloud Temple. The White Cloud Temple has numerous small statues within it **honoring** gods of many things, including the God of Rice, God of Riches, and God of Twins (a popular god since one of the ways around the one-child **limit** per family is to have twins). Visitors can **donate** money to the god from whom they need luck or help. There is also a bridge that is lined with huge copper **discs**. These discs have small openings in their centers containing bells. Tourists **purchase** discs to throw at the openings. Good luck comes to the person who succeeds in ringing the bell.

Answer in complete sentences:

1. What Mongol ruler founded Beijing?
2. Name one of the ruling dynasties of Beijing.
3. What is the Forbidden City?
4. Name a tourist attraction in Beijing.
5. How many children are the Chinese people allowed to have?

Web Sites:

http://www.chinavista.com/beijing/gugong/map.html
http://www.flashpaper.com/beijing/

Research

You will need:

- ✔ nonfiction books about China and the Forbidden City
- ✔ encyclopedia volume C
- ✔ paper
- ✔ pencil

Who was Pu Yi? Explain his story. Why was he important to Chinese history? Why was he driven out of the Forbidden City?

Language Arts

You will need:

- ✔ paper
- ✔ pencil

Write 10 proverbs you might find inside Chinese fortune cookies.

History

You will need:

- ✔ nonfiction information on Beijing
- ✔ paper
- ✔ pencil

Create a time line of the city of Beijing. Make sure that the most recent event you choose occurred at least 1,500 years after the earliest one happened.

Social Studies

You will need:

- ✔ nonfiction books about China
- ✔ Chinese cookbooks
- ✔ paper
- ✔ pencil

What are the basic foods in the Chinese diet? What Chinese foods have you eaten and enjoyed? Research and explain how rice is grown. Why is rice a main ingredient in most Chinese meals? In what other countries is rice the basic staple?

Giant Pandas

Use reference books or an encyclopedia to write a report about giant pandas. Use the following questions as a guide.

1. Describe the appearance of an adult giant panda. _____
   _____

2. What is the average height and weight of an adult? _____
   _____

3. What do pandas eat? How much do they eat? Why is it necessary for them to eat so often?
   _____
   _____

4. What is the panda's mating season?_____
   _____

5. Describe the appearance of a newborn panda. _____
   _____

6. Why are giant pandas endangered animals? _____
   _____

7. What is the Chinese government doing to protect the giant panda? _____
   _____

8. Why is it difficult to breed giant pandas in captivity?

   _____
   _____
   _____
   _____
   _____
   _____
   _____

Calcutta, India

Calcutta lies on the east bank of the Hooghly River, a branch of the Ganges River in eastern India. Calcutta was planned by the British to be like a European capital. It has highways leading to India's other major cities, railroad and subway systems, and an international airport. Many people depend on buses for local travel. Still, because of overpopulation, traffic jams are a common problem in downtown.

Maidan, in the center of the city, is a large, beautifully kept park. Major soccer, hockey, and cricket fields are located there. There are two race tracks and two golf courses in the city. Government buildings and expensive residences are near Maidan. This area has wide streets and modern housing. Some of India's wealthiest **residents** live in this section of Calcutta.

There is a huge difference between Calcutta's few rich residents and the rest of the extremely poor people. Most of the poor live in slums called *bustees* or live on the streets and beg for money. Many of the people in Calcutta are faced with problems of overcrowding, starvation, **unsanitary** conditions, and poverty. The Indian government is working to improve living conditions and control **outbreaks** of disease.

Other important attractions in Calcutta include the governor's residence, Raj Bhavan, the Victoria Memorial museums, and the Ochterlony Monument in Maidan Park. The Indian Museum is the oldest in the country and is called the "House of Magic" by the people of Calcutta. It displays examples of India's culture, including historic **artifacts** and crafts. It **features** an Egyptian mummy, a 200 million-year-old tree trunk, and some of the oldest **excavated relics** from the Indus Valley civilization.

Answer in complete sentences:

1. What is West Bengal?
2. Where is the Maidan located?
3. What are bustees?
4. Explain the transportation system of Calcutta.
5. What country designed Calcutta?

Web Site:
http://php.indiana.edu/~mduttara/wb/caltoc.html

Research

You will need:

- ✔ encyclopedia volume J
- ✔ paper
- ✔ pencil

Calcutta is the world center of jute production. What products are made from jute? In what form is jute exported from India? Explain the growing season and method of harvest.

Language Arts

You will need:

- ✔ paper
- ✔ pencil

City services are a problem in many parts of Calcutta. How would your life be different if your family had no garbage collection or sewer system? How does the lack of these services lead to health problems among the people of Calcutta?

Social Studies

You will need

- ✔ nonfiction information on Calcutta
- ✔ paper
- ✔ pencil

What government programs are needed to improve living conditions in Calcutta's *bustees*? Suggest five changes that would improve life for the people without sacrificing their traditions.

Social Studies

You will need

- ✔ nonfiction books about India's culture
- ✔ paper
- ✔ pencil

Explain how the festival of Divali is celebrated in the big cities of India.

Mother Teresa

For many years, the most famous resident of Calcutta was a Roman Catholic nun named Mother Teresa. She established the Missionaries of Charity religious order to care for the blind, aged, dying, and lepers in the poorest part of the city.

Mother Teresa was born in Albania in 1910 and began her training to be a nun in Ireland. When she arrived in Calcutta, she began working as a teacher at the convent school. She felt she was called to a ministry among the poor and suffering. Mother Teresa established the Missionaries of Charity, an order which grew to include 4,500 nuns working in 111 countries. In 1979, she was awarded the Nobel Peace Prize for her work in Calcutta. She later received the Bharat Ratna, India's highest civilian award.

In later years, serious health problems made it difficult for her to continue her work. Mother Teresa died on September 5, 1997, at her home in Calcutta. She was given a state funeral that was broadcast on television around the world.

Write an anecdote (story) from Mother Teresa's life.

Damascus, Syria

Damascus is one of the world's oldest cities. It is believed to be about 5,000 years old. Damascus was a part of the Greek, Roman, and Ottoman Empires at different times during its history. The country of Syria has a rich history with over 200 **archeological** and historical sites that are yet to be uncovered. All of Syria's conquerors and settlers have left their own individual marks on the country and given it a **diverse** cultural **heritage**. Today, most of the people of Damascus consider themselves Arabs.

Damascus is a desert **oasis** located in southwest Syria between the Anti-Lebanon Mountains and the Syrian Desert. The Barada River, which runs through Damascus, provides enough water for the residents. Because the amount of rainfall changes each year, Damascus has a system of providing running water from underground canals. Some of the stone walls that line the canals were built by the ancient Romans. Orchards of fruit trees must be **irrigated** in the dry months.

Modern Damascus lies north of the Barada River. Much of the city's business district was built during the French occupation in the 1900s. Today, this section has new office and high-rise apartment buildings. Its wide streets are crowded with traffic. The University of Damascus is outside the city.

Damascus is the center of **manufacturing** in Syria, not only of modern products and **wares**, but traditional crafts that the city made famous. Steel work in **damascene** designs is a centuries-old tradition which began in the Middle Ages when swords were made to be usable works of art. Handmade silk fabrics woven with silver and gold threads, called *damask,* are named after the city. They are not only beautiful with intricate designs, but are woven in a unique way that gives the fabric a raised **texture** on both sides of the cloth. **Bazaars** in the old section of the city display **handcrafted** glassware and wood carvings as well.

Answer in complete sentences:

1. What river brings water to the people of Damascus?
2. What is an oasis?
3. Where is the University of Damascus?
4. Describe the modern section of Damascus.
5. What is damask?

Web Sites:
http://www.geocities.com/SiliconValley/Lakes/2977/damas.html
http://www-personal.umich.edu/~kazamaza/syria.html

Language Arts

You will need:
- ✔ a book of folktales

Oral storytelling is traditional in Syria. Read one of the stories in a book of folktales and retell it aloud to a classmate using lots of details. When you have finished, ask the listener to draw a picture of one scene from the story.

Social Studies

You will need:
- ✔ nonfiction information about ancient trade routes
- ✔ paper
- ✔ pencil

Describe how people traveled through the desert 2,000 years ago. Describe how caravans travel today. Draw a sketch map and trace an ancient trade route.

Social Studies

You will need:
- ✔ international cookbooks
- ✔ paper
- ✔ pencil

Read several recipes for Middle Eastern foods. Prepare a snack of such items as hummus, pita, tabbouleh, and yogurt for the class to enjoy.

Art

You will need:
- ✔ scraps of construction paper
- ✔ scissors
- ✔ white glue
- ✔ glue stick
- ✔ poster board

Draw a geometric design on the poster board. Outline the design with white glue. Allow to dry. Cut pieces of paper scraps to fit inside the spaces of the design. Glue them in place using the glue stick.

The Ghutah Oasis

Desert oases are usually formed by underground springs that reach the surface in small pools. The water for the Ghutah Oasis, where Damascus is located, comes from the Barada River which flows out of the Anti-Lebanon Mountains. Along the coast of Syria at Damascus, there is enough rainfall to produce many crops.

The desert runs east of Damascus, through Syria, and into Jordan and Iraq. It is a rocky, barren desert. At certain times of the year, sandstorms blow across the desert into Damascus.

Research and answer:

1. Name the only navigable river in Syria._____

2. What crops are grown along the coast of Syria?_____

_____

3. What do nomads do during a drought? What do they do during a sandstorm?_____

_____

_____

_____

4. Name one other major world city that is built on an oasis. _____

Do two of the following projects:

1. Create a map showing Syria, Damascus, Aleppo, and the Barada and Euphrates Rivers.

2. Write a news story and headline about a sandstorm in Damascus.

3. Select one crop that is grown near Damascus. Explain how it is grown, harvested, and eaten. Draw pictures of the product before and after harvest.

Hanoi, Vietnam

The capital city of Vietnam is Ha Noi. *Ha* means river, referring to the Red River. *Noi* means inner or within. Together, the name means "city in the bend of the river." Hanoi has a unique combination of **classical** French buildings and wide tree-lined avenues with traditional Vietnamese **pagodas** and crowded street markets. It is also a city without any kind of suburbs. Once you cross the bridges that lead out of Hanoi, you find rice fields, dirt roads, and irrigation canals.

Long ago, Hanoi had 36 streets, or **guilds**, where merchants and **artisans** gathered to do business. The streets are named after the products or crafts that were sold on them. It is common for a street to have a **shrine** to the god of the trade for which it is named.

Three-wheeled taxis are one of the most common forms of public transportation in Hanoi. Another is called a *xich-lo* (pronounced SIK-loh). This is a three-wheeled cycle with a seat in front for a passenger or for **goods** and packages; the driver sits in back. Most people in Hanoi ride bicycles or **motor scooters**. Cars are not very commonly used, except by foreigners.

A famous Vietnamese landmark is the *Chua Mot Cot,* or the One Pillar Pagoda. It was built during the **reign** of King Ly Thai To (1028–1054). In a dream, the King **envisioned** the goddess Quan Am seated on a **lotus** leaf offering him a newborn male child. Shortly after that, the king married a peasant girl who bore a male **heir** to the throne. The king ordered the pagoda to be built as a sign of gratitude.

A popular form of entertainment is *Mua Roi Nuoc,* or Water Puppetry. It was created by farmers in **ancient** times who performed their shows in rice **paddie**s during the rainy season. Wooden puppets, controlled by puppeteers standing in waist-deep water behind a screen, act out a **skit** about life in rural Vietnam. They are **accompanied** by singers and a traditional orchestra.

Answer in complete sentences:

1. What is the meaning of the name Hanoi?
2. Explain the tradition of naming Hanoi's streets.
3. What king built the One Pillar Pagoda?
4. What is a xich-lo?
5. What is Mua Roi Nuoc?

Web Site:
http://www.vietscape.com/index.html

Research

You will need:
- ✔ nonfiction books on world religions
- ✔ encyclopedia volume B
- ✔ paper
- ✔ pencil

Write a brief summary of the teachings of Buddha. Explain the purpose of pagodas and temples in the practice of Buddhism.

Language Arts

You will need:
- ✔ encyclopedia volume V
- ✔ paper
- ✔ pencil
- ✔ supplies

Adapt information about life in rural Vietnam for a water puppet show. Design character puppets and write a brief dialog.

Music

You will need:
- ✔ nonfiction books about Vietnam and Eastern music
- ✔ paper
- ✔ pencil

Make drawings of three traditional Vietnamese musical instruments. Explain how each one similar or different to a Western instrument.

Social Studies

You will need:
- ✔ encyclopedia volumes H and V
- ✔ paper
- ✔ pencil

Draw a map showing the location of three Vietnamese cities: Hanoi, Haiphong, and Ho Chi Minh (Saigon). Include the latitude and longitude of each city. Explain how Hanoi and one of the other two cities are similar and different.

The One Pillar Pagoda

Retell the legend of the One Pillar Pagoda in your own words.

Hong Kong, China

Hong Kong lies near the mouth of the Pearl River, about 90 miles (145 km) southeast of Canton, China. For many years, it was a **colony** of Britain, but on July 1, 1997, the Chinese government took control of Hong Kong. It became a Special Administrative Region of the People's Republic of China. It is one of the most crowded cities in the world. Most of the people living in Hong Kong are Chinese and most of them work in factories, the shipping industry, or for the government. They may live in luxury apartments or low income high-rise apartment buildings. Many people live on boats in the **harbor** of the city.

One of the most important holidays to Hong Kongers is Chinese New Year. It occurs on the first lunar month of the year which is usually late January or February. To **ensure** good luck for the coming year, people are very careful with their activities the week before New Year's Eve. This includes paying off **debts**, cleaning the house, and mending friendships that may have gone **awry**. Homes are decorated with red- and gold-tasseled good luck charms. Tiny oranges are put on bushes. The streets are strung with lights and there is a huge fireworks display. At midnight, every light in the house is turned on to scare away evil spirits. On New Year's Day, absolutely no work is done, so as not to **hex** any good luck.

Skyscrapers fill the crowded business district of Hong Kong. There is little green space like parks or reserves. **Developers** who want to expand the city must **reclaim** land from the sea. A new international airport was created by **leveling** a small, uninhabited island, *Chek Lap Kok*. Many city **dwellers** enjoy outdoor activities and the natural beauty of nearby fishing villages and **undeveloped** islands.

Answer in complete sentences:

1. What is Chinese New Year?
2. When did the Chinese government take control of Hong Kong?
3. How many islands make up Hong Kong?
4. Why must developers reclaim land from the sea?
5. Where is Hong Kong located?

Web Sites:

http://www.yahoo.com.sg/docs/features/hk97/
http://www.hk1997.china.com/english/front/front.html

Research

You will need:
- ✓ nonfiction information about Hong Kong
- ✓ paper
- ✓ pencil

Explain the topography of Hong Kong. Why must the people live in a small area? Draw a topographical map of the region. Be sure to include a map key.

Research

You will need:
- ✓ nonfiction information about marine life (dolphins)
- ✓ paper
- ✓ pencil

The Chinese white dolphin is being driven to extinction because of work in the South China Sea to build the Chek Lap Kok Airport. In what other parts of the world does this dolphin live? What could be done to help the dolphins' survival?

Language Arts

You will need:
- ✓ paper
- ✓ pencil

Pretend you are a citizen of Hong Kong. Write a journal entry for June 30, 1997, telling how you feel on the day before the handover. What (if any) are your concerns?

Social Studies

You will need:
- ✓ tourist information about Hong Kong
- ✓ nonfiction information about Chinese culture
- ✓ paper
- ✓ pencil

The Museum of Tea Ware has displays of items used to serve tea. Research and explain the history and importance of tea in the Chinese culture.

Hong Kong, China

Chek Lap Kok Airport

The construction of a new, world-class airport at Chek Lap Kok is the largest single construction project ever undertaken in Hong Kong. A small, rocky island was leveled to create the land for the airport. Additional land was reclaimed to build a railway to the airport. The airport operates around the clock with a capacity of up to 35 million passengers and 3 million tons of cargo a year.

Read about the Kansai Airport (Osaka, Japan). It was built on an artificial island. Explain two ways this airport is like the Chek Lap Kok Airport.

1. _____

   _____

2. _____

   _____

The Tsing Ma Bridge

The Tsing Ma Bridge is one of the world's longest suspension bridges, carrying both road and rail traffic to the islands of Tsing Yi and Ma Wan. The bridge was opened in an explosion of fireworks by former British Prime Minister Margaret Thatcher on Sunday, April 27, 1997.

Name five other world cities that have suspension bridges. Complete this chart.

Bridge	City	River
_____	_____	_____
_____	_____	_____
_____	_____	_____
_____	_____	_____
_____	_____	_____

The Hong Kong Convention and Exhibition Centre

The Hong Kong Convention and Exhibition Centre, a new landmark on Hong Kong's harbor, was the site of the Hong Kong Handover Ceremony. With its distinctive curved roof, the Centre is a symbol of Hong Kong's future as Asia's international business hub. The Centre is an international business facility, with restaurants, cafes, and an underground parking garage.

On the back of this paper, explain the general purpose of convention centers around the world. List five services they provide. If there is a convention center in your city, call it and make a list of the current exhibits.

Isfahan, Iran

Isfahan is in the center of Iran, about 200 miles (322 km) south of Tehran, the capital. Iran has one of the largest oil deposits in the world, making it a very **prosperous** country. Iran has wisely spent the money on improving its schools, universities, health services, and other technological advances. Isfahan **boasts** the grandest architecture in the country. **Mosques**, palaces, and temples give the city an elegant beauty.

Isfahan is not the capital of Iran, today, but it was the capital of the great Persian Empire when it was ruled by Shah Abbas. The Siosepol Bridge over the Zayandel River was built by Shah Abbas. This beautiful bridge has 33 **arches** supporting the roadway as well as 100 smaller arches that create **arcades** above the road.

The center of Isfahan is called Imam Square. The square is surrounded by many beautiful buildings including the famous blue-domed Imam Mosque. Another mosque, the Lotfollah Mosque, has **glazed tiles** of turquoise, yellow, and pink that create delicate **swirling** animal and floral patterns. The Friday's Mosque, one of the oldest in Isfahan, has a large central courtyard and a marble **reflecting** pool which promotes the quiet **meditative** prayer that occurs at the mosque. Blue-roofed domes top most of Isfahan's mosques and flow **vividly** out among the brown hills surrounding Isfahan.

Isfahan has always been well known for its excellent artisans and artists. The walls of many **structures** are covered with hand-painted scenes of Persian history in fine **detail**. Products made in Isfahan include **textiles**, **brocades**, **lacquerware**, and other handmade goods like rugs and silver jewelry. These are sold at huge outdoor **bazaars**. Intricately woven Iranian carpets sell for tens of thousands of dollars and are passed down as family **heirlooms**.

Answer in complete sentences:

1. Name the capital city of Iran.
2. When did Shah Abbas rule Persia?
3. Describe the Siosepol Bridge.
4. Name two mosques in Isfahan.
5. What kinds of work are done by people living in Isfahan?

Web Site:
http://persia.org/imagemap/esfahan.html

Research

You will need:
- ✔ nonfiction information about Islam
- ✔ paper
- ✔ pencil

Research the Shiite branch of Islam. What are their specific beliefs? How do they differ from Sunni Moslems? Who are the *mujtahid*, the *mullah*, and the *ayatollah*?

Research

You will need:
- ✔ cookbooks
- ✔ paper
- ✔ pencil

Locate three recipes that use either apricots or pistachio nuts as a main ingredient. Write one of them. If possible, bring a snack of dried apricots or pistachio nuts to share with the class.

Language Arts

You will need:
- ✔ paper
- ✔ pencil

Newspapers and television are controlled by the government of Iran. What kinds of information would probably NOT be given the people under that system? Explain how government control of the media affects the daily life of the Iranian people. What does freedom of speech mean to you?

Social Studies

You will need:
- ✔ encyclopedia volume P
- ✔ paper
- ✔ pencil

Create a time line of six important events that occurred during the Persian Dynasties.

Isfahan, Iran

Match each word to its synonym.

_____ 1. kingdom   a. statue

_____ 2. textiles   b. garden

_____ 3. rugs   c. round ceiling

_____ 4. mosque   d. place of worship

_____ 5. arch   e. fabrics

_____ 6. dome   f. empire

_____ 7. brocade   g. carpets

_____ 8. courtyard   h. curved opening

_____ 9. shah   i. embroidered fabric

_____ 10. monument   j. ruler

_____ 11. minaret   k. tower

Label the following pictures with these words:
minaret, mosque, dome, courtyard, reflecting pool

_____ _____ _____

_____ _____

Jakarta, Indonesia

Indonesia is the world's largest **archipelago**, a nation of more than 10,000 islands and **islets**. More than half of them are uninhabited. The outer islands are mostly rain forest areas and have hundreds of volcanoes located on them. There is usually at least one major **eruption** each year, causing great destruction. However, the eruptions cause the inner islands of Bali, Java, and others to gain more **fertile** soil. So, the deadly volcanoes actually provide the rest of the country with some of the richest tropical soil in the world.

Jakarta began as a trading **port**. It was a small, walled village built to look like a **scaled-down** Amsterdam, today's capital of the Netherlands. The Dutch East India Company controlled the island port as the town became rich from spice **exports**. The Dutch named the city Batavia. Indonesia won its independence in 1946 and Batavia was renamed Jakarta.

Jakarta is an industrial city with only a few skyscrapers and highways. Most of the city consists of one- and two-story buildings and narrow streets. Wealthy people live in a section called *Menteng*. The houses in *Menteng* were built during the time the Dutch ruled the **colony**. More than half of Jakartans live in small homes made of **bamboo** and have no electricity.

Indonesia is well known for its handmade fabrics. Javanese **batik** is especially famous. The process involves painting with a wax substance which **resists** dye. Then, the fabric is dipped into different colors of dyes. The painted patterns are usually **symbolic**, with special designs for weddings and other events. Ikat weaving is another popular textile craft in Indonesia's eastern islands. The colors **vary** and the patterns are bolder and simpler than batik patterns. The fabric is made into a **sarong** which is tied around the waist into a long skirt. Ikat cloth's colors and patterns are also symbolic like the batiks. Some designs are thought to have power and magic or are used in ceremonies to protect the wearer from illness.

Answer in complete sentences:

1. How many islands and islets are in the Indonesian archipelago?
2. What is Batavia?
3. What European country claimed Indonesia as a colony?
4. When did Indonesia win its independence?
5. What is batik?

Web Site:
http://discover-jakarta.com/

Science

You will need:
- ✔ nonfiction information about Indonesia
- ✔ paper
- ✔ pencil

How have volcanoes affected the topography and agriculture of Indonesia? Where are the Krakatoa and Gunung Agung volcanoes located?

Science

You will need:
- ✔ nonfiction information about Indonesia
- ✔ paper
- ✔ pencil

What is a *rafflesia?* Describe it and make a drawing.

Geography

You will need:
- ✔ map of Indonesia
- ✔ white drawing paper
- ✔ pencil

Make a map of Indonesia with the islands of Borneo, New Guinea, Sumatra, Java, Bali, and Sulawasi. Label Jakarta. Label examples of an archipelago, islet, island, and peninsula.

Art

You will need:
- ✔ tagboard
- ✔ hole punch
- ✔ paper fasteners
- ✔ markers
- ✔ plastic drinking straws
- ✔ scissors

Create your own shadow puppet. From tagboard, cut the puppet with detached arms. Color it. Using the hole punch, attach the arms loosely with the paper fasteners. Tape a straw on each arm.

Wayang Kulit (Shadow Puppetry)

Puppet shows are a traditional form of Indonesian theater. The shows are performed for special occasions like festivals or celebrations. Performances may last for two or three days, continuing all night long. The stories are based on Indonesian folktales or themes from the Hindu religion. They are presented by a *dalang,* or puppeteer.

A master *dalang* must learn to tell the stories in two or three languages, work all the puppets, and create different voices for each of the characters. The *dalang* performs from behind a screen.

The *wayangs* (puppets) do not look exactly like people because the Islamic religion does not allow art that uses figures of men or women. The puppets are detailed paper dolls of odd-looking creatures. They are moved about in front of a light to cast shadows on a screen between the *dalang* and the audience.

Wayang Kulit Puppet Theater

You will need:
- ✔ large cardboard box
- ✔ ruler
- ✔ pencil
- ✔ box cutter or sharp scissors
- ✔ gauze or thin white cloth (to cover the opening in the box)
- ✔ masking tape
- ✔ small lamp

Directions:
1. Measure and draw a line around all four sides of the box bottom 2 inches (5 cm) in from the edge.
2. Ask an adult to help you use scissors to cut on the line. Remove the bottom of the box.
3. Cut the fabric to fit the opening. Tape it firmly over the opening on all four sides.
4. Prepare your puppets. Plan your story and movements.
5. Plug in the light. Let it shine on the screen from behind.
6. Perform your puppet show from behind the screen with the light shining behind the puppets.

Jerusalem, Israel

Jerusalem is the capital of Israel and a holy city for three major religions. Christians believe Jerusalem is holy because it is the place where Jesus lived and was **crucified.** For Jews, the city has been their **eternal** capital since Biblical times. Muslims believe that Muhammad went up to heaven from Jerusalem. It is also, historically, an important location for trade routes between East and West, making Jerusalem a much sought-after territory. Surviving century after century of war and unrest, this ancient, sacred city has a **depth** and mystery all its own.

The city was divided between Israel and Jordan in 1948. Israel won control of East Jerusalem during the Six Day War in 1967, after which the Israeli government was able to open the gates of the Old City so that everyone could visit the holy places. The Western Wall is all that remains of a Jewish temple destroyed by the Romans in A.D. 70. The Church of the Holy Sepulcher stands on Calvary, the hill where Jesus was crucified. The Dome of the Rock is built over the rock from which Muhammad **ascended** to heaven.

The Old City is surrounded by a high stone wall. There are no modern industries in this section of Jerusalem. The narrow **cobblestone** streets are lined with markets and shops selling farm products, souvenirs, food items, and **handicrafts**. The modern world is almost left behind when you enter the gates leading to the Old City. Where else in the world can you play video games in an **arcade** with Byzantine arches, buy vegetables in a market held up with Roman **columns**, or take a **spa** in a 1,000-year-old bathhouse once inhabited by the Crusaders?

West Jerusalem has modern factories, large housing projects, and office buildings. New Jerusalem blends easily with the old as there is little glass and steel construction. A law from the early part of this century declares that all buildings be built with Jerusalem's famous sandy-gold stone.

Answer in complete sentences:

1. What three religious groups consider Jerusalem to be their holy city?
2. Name three holy places in the Old City.
3. What two countries fought in the Six Day War of 1967?
4. What are the main differences between daily life in West Jerusalem and the Old City?
5. Where in Israel is Jerusalem?

Web Sites:
http://jeru.huji.ac.il/jerusalem.html
http://www.israel-mfa.gov.il/mfa/capital/jlemmain.html

Research

You will need:

- ✔ encyclopedia volume J
- ✔ pencil
- ✔ paper

Explain how each of Jerusalem's three religious groups observes their Sabbath.

History

You will need:

- ✔ nonfiction information on architecture in Jerusalem
- ✔ encyclopedia volume J
- ✔ pencil
- ✔ paper

Write a paragraph describing the ancient underground water system in Jerusalem. *Hint:* Use newspapers and magazines to research recent discoveries by archaeologists.

Language Arts

You will need:

- ✔ encyclopedia volume J
- ✔ travel brochures
- ✔ pencil
- ✔ paper

Choose a holy place to research. Write a journal entry or postcard telling about your experiences visiting the location.

Social Studies

You will need:

- ✔ encyclopedia volume J (Jerusalem) and W (Western Wall)
- ✔ paper
- ✔ pencil

Explain the religious significance of the Western Wall, the Church of the Holy Sepulcher, and the Dome of the Rock.

Jerusalem, Israel

Word Search Puzzle

```
H A E O L R E T E T I Y S O D S A E
E E N L U R A N O D T E S D A P I E
E B I B L I C A L I H E T G F A T R
D T E R M H A H C C N N O O S E N C
O T I I O L E D R E L I G I O N S O
C D N A H A L A A U C L E E U E E B
A D O M E O F T H E R O C K C T E B
L D I B W E L C Y M C A E E R N E L
V O S R Y E M Y E I R E R O U D I E
A A E T S Z S L S R C Y I C S R S S
R C T H N I A T M E O A I A A T R T
Y A A E O S X N E U P M Z S D D A O
U A U P U L R D T R H U A I E C E N
B Y G R I S Y N A I N A L N R U L E
V I E E O T M C A Y N W M C S B G A
C J W A R S A A I H W E A M H H D E
O T H L E S D L E T H A E L A E S E
D X S H L F I Y T E Y E R T L D R N
```

Look for these words:

JERUSALEM

WESTERN WALL

DOME OF THE ROCK

CALVARY

SPA

CRUSADERS

RELIGIONS

ROMANS

OLD CITY

CAPITAL

SIX DAY WAR

HOLY SEPULCHER

BIBLICAL

BYZANTINE

ARCHES

HOLY CITY

MUHAMMAD

COBBLESTONE

ARCADE

ISRAEL

Kuala Lumpur, Malaysia

Kuala Lumpur, the largest city in Malaysia, began as a small **settlement** near a rich tin mine. It is located on the **banks** of the Klang and Gombak Rivers in the southern part of the Malay Peninsula. The British **invested** in the area because of its location as a southeastern seaport. Kuala Lumpur grew quickly as many Chinese moved into the area to work in the tin mines. Soon it was discovered that the islands had perfect conditions for growing rubber and coffee. Workers from India moved to Malaysia to work on the plantations. Taxes from tin, rubber, and coffee provided money to run the country. Today, KL, as it is called, is a modern city that **values** Asian traditions.

The heart of KL is Merdeka Square, a park lined with government buildings. Sultan Abdul Samed Building, topped by a 141-foot (43-m) clock tower and shiny copper domes, is in the square. The Masjid Jame (Friday Mosque), with its silvery domes and pink and white **minarets**, is surrounded by palm trees and overlooks the square. KL also has some of the most modern buildings in the world. The 88-story Petronas Twin Towers, part of the new Kuala Lumpur City Centre, are among the world's tallest buildings.

To the south of Merdeka Square is Chinatown, a colorful area that features a busy night market. Petaling Street and Jalan Bandar are the city's main shopping streets. A variety of textiles, clothes, jewelry, shoes, and handbags are available at bargain prices. **Stalls** selling tea, **herbs**, spices, fruits, **incense**, and more unusual items like sharks' fins also crowd the streets. Along Jalan Melaka and Jalan Masjid India, known as "Little India," there are some unique **vendors** spread out on the sidewalks. They are **flamboyant** medicine men who **operate** a sort of street-side clinic. They supposedly cure anything from skin rashes to cobra bites. This **alternative** medicine uses plants, dried herbs, barks, and oils.

Answer in complete sentences:

1. Where is Kuala Lumpur located?
2. Name three products that were important to the early development of the area.
3. Name a river in Kuala Lumpur.
4. Name the city's main shopping streets.
5. Name three of the world's tallest skyscrapers.

Web Sites:

http://asiatravel.com/kuainfo.html
http://www.mnet.com.my/klonline/

Research

You will need:

✔ nonfiction information about Malaysia
✔ paper
✔ pencil

What are *satay? durians?* How are they prepared and eaten?

Social Studies

You will need:

✔ nonfiction information about Malaysia
✔ paper
✔ pencil

Explain the relationship that exists among the Malaysian, Chinese, and Indian populations in Malaysia, today.

Art

You will need:

✔ markers
✔ scissors
✔ tagboard
✔ ribbons
✔ art supplies (to decorate the kites)

Design a large kite. Cut out the shape, decorate it, and hang it from the ceiling of your classroom.

Sports

You will need:

✔ small foam rubber ball

Try the Malaysian game of *sepak raga.* Players stand in a circle and keep the ball in motion without touching it with their hands. The ball may be hit with feet, knees, elbows, or heads.

Malaysian Industries

Do research on one of the following topics, then write a paragraph describing that industry in Malaysia.

▲ tin mining   ▲ rubber
▲ coffee   ▲ palm oil

Mumbai (Bombay), India

Bombay has been renamed Mumbai. The word comes from the name *Mumbadevi*, the patron goddess of the Koli fisherfolk who were the earliest **inhabitants** of Bombay. The idea of returning to the older ways, or the roots, of Indian life is a popular one, today—especially in India's cities. The traditional arts are experiencing a new **trend** of acceptance, as this is a city where old ways combine with modern city living. Mumbai is the capital of the state of Maharashtra and the largest and most modern **metropolitan** area in India. Located on an island just off the west coast of India, Mumbai is also the country's major port and most important **industrial** city.

Because of its location and history as a Portuguese and British trading port, Mumbai is a world trading center. Cotton **textiles** and clothing are among the most important exports. Like many other Indian crafts and art, these fabrics have **intricate** floral and animal designs. The textile industry employs about half of Bombay's workers.

One cannot experience India without experiencing its religions. Hinduism is the most common religion in India. It is a way of life and can be seen in the country's art, architecture, and customs. Besides promoting peace, nonviolence, and truth, Hinduism holds many things sacred. Cows are considered very holy and are worshiped. They are thought to be the givers of life-sustaining milk and symbols of **fertility.** Therefore, eating beef is **taboo.** Many other animals are associated with different gods. This is why many Hindus are vegetarians.

In India, people practice a variety of religions in addition to Hinduism, including Islam, Christianity, Buddhism, Sikhism, and Jainism. Many practices of these religions involve food **preferences** and fasting. Some religious ceremonies require fasting for certain periods of time. For many, a spiritual life requires a **disciplined** diet.

Answer in complete sentences:

1. Where in India is Mumbai?
2. What is the new name of Bombay and what does it mean?
3. What does it mean to be vegetarian?
4. What is Bombay's most important industry?
5. Why are many Hindu people vegetarians?

Web Sites:
http://theory.tifr.res.in/bombay/
http://www.mumbainet.com/

Research

You will need:
- ✔ paper
- ✔ pencil

Bombay produces and exports cotton fabrics and clothing. Brainstorm a list of jobs related to the textile industry. Include all the work done from the time cotton is picked until a garment is offered for sale.

Research

You will need:
- ✔ encyclopedia volume G
- ✔ paper
- ✔ pencil

Mohandas Gandhi was born in 1869 near Bombay. Explain his belief in nonviolence and how he led the people of India to challenge British authority.

Geography

You will need:
- ✔ world atlas
- ✔ encyclopedia volume S (Suez Canal)
- ✔ paper
- ✔ pencil
- ✔ worksheet on page 67

How did the opening of the Suez Canal affect Bombay's economy? Trace the shipping route from India to Europe on a map. (See page 67.)

Social Studies

You will need:
- ✔ nonfiction books about India's culture
- ✔ paper
- ✔ pencil

Explain how the festival of Holi (spring) is celebrated in the big cities of India.

Suez Canal

1. Trace the shipping route from Mumbai to a destination in Europe via the Suez Canal.

2. Name the bodies of water crossed and three southern European countries.

_____

_____

_____

3. Explain how the Suez Canal changed trade coming from Mumbai.

_____

_____

_____

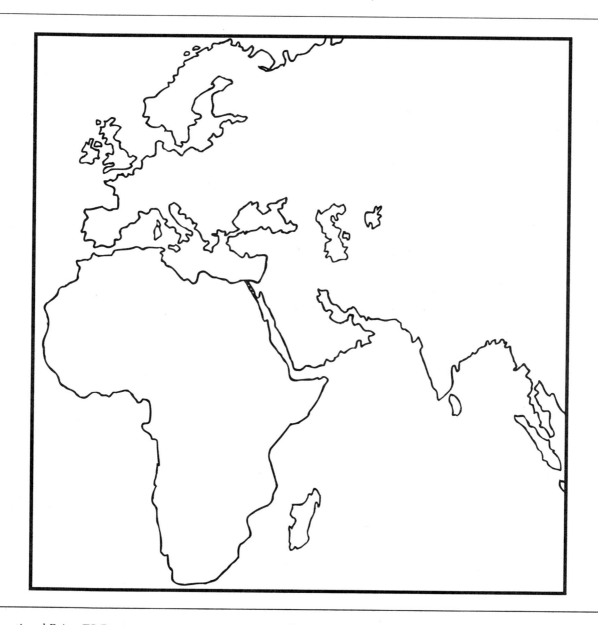

Seoul, Korea

Seoul is located on the northwest of the Korean Peninsula, east of the Yellow Sea. The Han River **flows** through the city, dividing it into two sections. The name Seoul comes from the Korean word ***sorabol***, meaning "the center of everything." It is the capital of South Korea and one of the 10 largest cities in the world. Over the centuries, Korea has been **invaded** and **occupied** by China and Japan. The Japanese built many Western-style buildings and roads, and destroyed many Korean palaces and some of the country's oldest **structures**. After Japan lost World War II, Korea was divided into two separate governments. The communists of the Soviet Union ran the North and the United States military ran the South. Because of its location at the center of the **peninsula**, Seoul is very near the Demilitarized Zone (DMZ). People cannot travel freely between the two countries.

Like many war-torn cities, Seoul has a combination of old and new architecture. Old palaces have been **preserved** or rebuilt and are now open as art and history museums. Changdok Palace and its nearby Secret Garden are among the best known. Kyongbok Palace and Toksu Palace are also in the city and have served as royal residences as far back as the 15th century. Many of the palaces have beautiful **frescoes** featuring plant and animal life.

There are four major religions practiced in Korea: Buddhism and Confucianism, both of which come from China, Shamanism, and Christianity. Shamanism is not an organized religion with temples and sacred scripture. Its **practitioners** have been **persecuted** for centuries and yet it is still a strong force in Korea. Shamanism's spiritual leaders are called *mudangs,* and are usually women. This may be one reason they are not accepted by the mostly male-dominated religions like Confucianism. The mudang's role is to "speak" to the spirit world in order to assist the living with problems, illness, or even **safe-guarding** an entire village. They **conduct** ceremonies that include song, dance, and prayer where the *mudang* uses **cymbals** and drums to communicate with the spirit world.

Answer in complete sentences:

1. What is the DMZ?
2. Who controls North Korea? South Korea?
3. Where is the Secret Garden?
4. What is a mudang?
5. Name two religions practiced in Korea.

Web Sites:
http://www.city.net/countries/south_korea/seoul/
http://www.metro.seoul.kr/

Language Arts

You will need:

✔ nonfiction books about Korea
✔ paper
✔ pencil

If you were a child growing up in a traditional Korean home, how would you behave towards your father? Your mother? How are the roles of men and women determined by religion?

Social Studies

You will need:

✔ map of Korea
✔ nonfiction information about Korea
✔ encyclopedia volume K
✔ paper
✔ pencil

Copy the map of Korea, label Seoul, and draw the DMZ between the North and South. Write a paragraph explaining the structure and purpose of the Demilitarized Zone.

Art

You will need:

✔ art supplies

Design a kite that might be flown at Children's Park in Seoul to celebrate Children's Day, a spring holiday.

Art

You will need:

✔ paper
✔ pencil
✔ colored pencils or crayons

Make labeled drawings of men's and women's *hanbok*, traditional Korean costumes.

Seoul, Korea

Crossword Puzzle

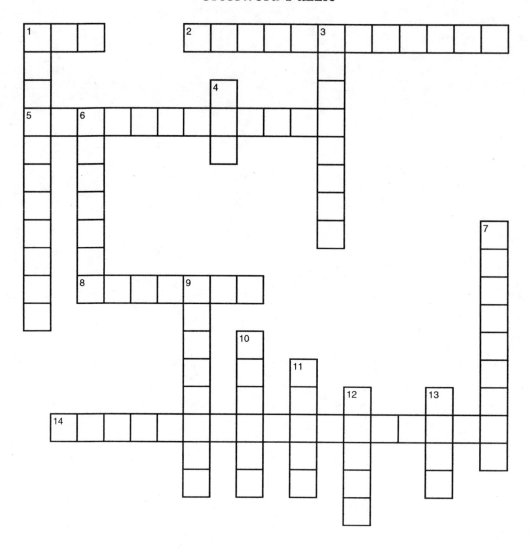

ACROSS

1. Number of governments in Korea after World War II
2. A male-dominated religion
5. Located near Changdok Palace
8. Korean name for Seoul
14. What DMZ stands for

DOWN

1. Royal Residence in Seoul
3. Museum that used to be a palace
4. River in Seoul
6. Instrument used by *mudangs* to communicate with spirit world
7. Seoul is located east of the ___.
9. Korean religion that came from China
10. Female leader in Shamanism
11. Country other than Japan that invaded Korea in the past
12. Capital of South Korea
13. Number of major religions practiced in Korea

Shanghai, China

Shanghai is China's largest city and an important trading port. It is on the Huangpu River at the mouth of the Yangtze River. Shanghai began as a small trading village. In 1842, Britain forced China to open its ports to foreign trade and people from several European countries moved to the city. These people built homes, churches, and office buildings that gave Shanghai the look of a European city.

China is a **socialist** country, today, and tries to discourage Western **influences**. However, since 1979, socialist **policies** have changed to allow some foreign **investment** in China. People are **permitted** to own small businesses like restaurants, repair shops, and laundries. In this way, the government is hoping to improve the **unemployment** rate and make **goods** and services more **available** to the people of Shanghai.

Shanghai is a city with many industries and manufacturing centers that grew very quickly. Because of overcrowding and industrial development, air and water pollution are very serious problems in Shanghai. Waste dumped into the Huangpu River and high levels of **sulfur dioxide** in the air make the environment a threat to people's health.

In spite of the problems of a big city, Shanghai is an exciting place to visit. The main shopping street in Shanghai is Nanjing Road. Bright with **neon** lights, it has most of the city's department stores, the largest of which is called Number One Department Store. In the Old Town, the traditional Chinese Yu Garden **exhibits** a beautiful and peaceful **labyrinth** of **lotus** ponds with goldfish, **pavilions**, winding paths, towers, and **pagodas**. At the entrance of Yu Garden is the Huxinting Teahouse which stands in the middle of a rectangular pool. This five-sided pavilion is the perfect resting spot to sip tea and watch the many passersby.

Answer in complete sentences:

1. Explain the location of Shanghai.
2. What is Nanjing Road?
3. Why is the Huangpu River polluted?
4. Why does Shanghai have many European-style buildings?
5. How have socialist policies changed since 1979?

Web Sites:

http://www.chinats.com/cshangh.htm
http://shanghai.mzn.com/
http://china-window.com/shanghai/shbf/eindex.html

Research

You will need:
- nonfiction information about China and Shanghai
- paper
- pencil

Who was Mao Tse-Tung? How did the cultural revolution affect the Shanghai government?

Geography

You will need:
- map of China
- paper
- pencil

Draw a sketch map showing the location of Shanghai, the Huangpu and Yangtze Rivers, and the East China Sea.

Social Studies

You will need:
- nonfiction information about sports
- paper
- pencil

Explain the rules and scoring for China's favorite sports, volleyball and table tennis (ping pong).

Art

You will need:
- paper
- ink or watercolors
- fine paintbrush

Traditional Chinese art depicts nature or landscapes. Look at some examples of Chinese paintings. Create a picture in the same style.

Shanghai's Future

Shanghai is preparing to be a world financial and trade center in the coming century. The city has a long term plan for social and economic development.

City leaders believe that it will be necessary to:

▲ modernize the city's transportation system, including the airports, seaports, light rail system, and roads

▲ make the Shanghai Stock Exchange one of the main Asian stock markets

▲ improve the education system

▲ improve public health care

▲ create a social security system

▲ attract economic investment from outside China

▲ reduce air and water pollution

▲ increase the life expectancy of residents to 76.5 years

▲ begin a national fitness program

▲ create an international market for Shanghai's products

▲ maintain an average annual wage increase of 3–5% in employees' salaries

Which items directly affect Shanghai's people?
1. _____
2. _____
3. _____
4. _____
5. _____

Which items helps to build Shanghai's economy?
1. _____
2. _____
3. _____
4. _____
5. _____

Bonus: Answer on the back of this paper. How does building the economy help the people living in Shanghai?

Singapore, Singapore

The capital of the country of Singapore is the city of Singapore, located on the southern tip of the Malay Peninsula. Almost all of the people in this small country live in the capital city. Most of them are Chinese, Malay, Indian, or British. Singapore is made up of one large island and about fifty smaller ones. It is one of the most **prosperous** Asian countries.

The city is built around a large harbor. Singapore is a free port where goods are unloaded, stored, and shipped without payment of import **duties**, which helps to make it one of the world's busiest ports. Factories in Singapore **produce** electronic equipment, metals, paper, rubber, scientific instruments, **textiles**, and clothing. Shipbuilding and fishing are important industries. There is little unemployment in Singapore.

Singapore is sometimes called the "Garden City" because its tropical climate makes it easy to grow a wide **variety** of **exotic** flowers and plants. **Lush** trees, bushes, and colorful flowers grow **amid** a tropical rain forest background. The Botanical Gardens, the Zoological Gardens which **maintain** one of the largest colonies of orangutans, and Jurong Bird Park are popular tourist attractions maintained by the government.

Singaporeans enjoy many cultural and **recreational** activities. Because of its location, boat races are common. A popular event in many Asian countries is the Dragon Boat Festival. This race honors a famous Chinese poet who drowned himself to protest a **corrupt** government. Brightly decorated boats shaped like dragons are raced across the waters of East Coast Parkway. The crew includes at least 24 rowers and a drummer who sets the pace. The festival, held at the end of May, includes a celebration where people enjoy a **feast** of rice dumplings stuffed with meat and wrapped in bamboo leaves.

Answer in complete sentences:

1. Where is Singapore?
2. What is meant by the name "Garden City"?
3. What is a free port?
4. Name an industry of Singapore.
5. What four nationalities make up the population of Singapore?

Web Site:
http://www.focus-asia.com/home/kenghor/postcard/postcard1.html

Research

You will need:
- ✔ nonfiction information about Singapore
- ✔ paper
- ✔ pencil

Explain the Singapore songbird contests. How are they organized? How are the birds judged? Why are songbirds popular pets in Singapore?

Language Arts

You will need:
- ✔ paper
- ✔ pencil

Singapore is a popular tourist destination. Write a letter to a friend giving at least five reasons why he or she should travel to Singapore.

Social Studies

You will need:
- ✔ nonfiction information about Singapore
- ✔ paper
- ✔ pencil

Singaporeans celebrate many festivals throughout the year. Choose one to describe in detail. Make a year-long calendar of celebrations. Indicate the culture group associated with each one.

Science

You will need:
- ✔ nonfiction information about exotic plants and flowers
- ✔ paper
- ✔ pencil

Many orchids are grown and exported from Singapore. What conditions are best for raising orchids? For what are they used?

Land Reclamation

Land reclamation is an important activity in Singapore. It provides jobs and expands the size of the city. Most new construction in Singapore has been high-rise buildings and skyscrapers. Now, the only way the city can grow is to reclaim areas of the sea. Almost every hill in the city has been cut down. The soil from the hills has been used to fill in where there was once water. Sand is being dredged from the sea and landfill is being taken from the offshore islands for new projects.

Reclaimed land makes up about half of the Changi International Airport. Marine Square, containing three hotels and a shopping center, and the East Coast Park are both built on constructed land.

Research and answer these questions:

1. Why are there few hills left in Singapore? _____

   _____

2. How are the offshore islands helping with land reclamation? _____

   _____

3. What projects have been built on reclaimed land? _____

   _____

4. Why must much of Singapore's construction be "built up"? _____

   _____

5. What jobs are created for Singaporeans because of the need to reclaim land? _____

   _____

6. What heavy equipment is used in land reclamation projects? _____

   _____

7. Name two other cities in the world that reclaim land from the sea. What characteristics do those cities have in common with Singapore?

   _____

   _____

   _____

   _____

   _____

   _____

   _____

Sydney, Australia

In 1787, Captain Arthur Phillip sailed from England with more than 1,000 **convicts**. Prisons were overcrowded in England and British officials believed that making a prison colony in Australia was a good way to solve the problem. Captain Phillip landed at The Rocks in Sydney Harbor a year later. The Rocks soon became a small village that was extremely dangerous. Knife fights and robberies were common among the **thugs** who inhabited the crowded **maze** of narrow streets. Most of the oldest buildings that made up The Rocks were destroyed after an **outbreak** of the **bubonic plague** in 1900. What exists today is a small, restored suburb with **quaint** shops and cafes that was rebuilt after the **disease-ridden** streets were cleaned up. It is one of the city's most popular tourist attractions.

The Sydney Opera House, completed in 1973, is the most famous landmark in the city. This **futuristic** structure was designed to look like the sails of a **clipper ship** floating gracefully in the harbor. The white roofs (sails) of the building contain more than 1 million Swedish **tiles**. The opera house is actually an arts **complex** with **galleries**, concert halls, theaters, and restaurants. It is one of the world's most recognized buildings.

Residents of Sydney are called *Sydneysiders*. Most of them are able to own a home, but the rising cost of land is making home ownership more difficult for young people. This is a country of vast space. New South Wales is home to only 5.9 million people, less than the **population** of London alone. This is one of the reasons Sydney is a **popular** city for **immigrants** from all over the world. People are moving to Sydney in **droves**. It is not uncommon to see signs in four or five different languages all over the city. The mild climate also makes this an **irresistible** place. Sydneysiders enjoy outdoor sports like sailing, swimming, and waterskiing. The many gorgeous beaches around Sydney are famous for surf **enthusiasts**.

Answer in complete sentences:

1. Why did the British establish a colony in Australia?
2. What are The Rocks?
3. Describe Sydney's Opera House.
4. Where in Australia is New South Wales? Sydney?
5. What outdoor sports are enjoyed by Sydney residents?

Web Sites:
http://www.sydney.com.au/
http://www.city.net/countries/australia/new_south_wales/sydney

Research

You will need:
- ✔ nonfiction books on Australia
- ✔ paper
- ✔ pencil

Research information about another of Australia's major cities. Compare and contrast that city with Sydney.

Language Arts

You will need:
- ✔ nonfiction books on Australia
- ✔ paper
- ✔ pencil

When is Australia Day? How is it celebrated? Design a greeting card for this important holiday.

Social Studies

You will need:
- ✔ reference books on sports
- ✔ paper
- ✔ pencil

In Australia, the major team sport in the summer is cricket. Rugby, a kind of football, is another favorite sport. Explain the rules for cricket or rugby.

Music

You will need:
- ✔ reference materials on classical music
- ✔ paper
- ✔ pencil

Create a classical symphony program that might be presented at the Sydney Opera House. Include the works of at least three different composers.

Sydney, Australia

Word Search Puzzle

```
C O L O N Y V G A L L E R I E S O M
P O B E O N O S A L A N D M A R K A
E U U N E W S O U T H W A L E S I O
H S B A S S A I L I N G N P N L A D
C Y O S A S C M O O S C I E A I R F
H D N N F L E R T T E L P R A O T U
N N I I S L D A C L L P T G U T S T
R E C L N T A I I I I S N E E E C U
E Y P F C E V I H H U I T T D E O R
R S L A R N D P S A I F D E N O M I
T I A S O E N R E K N N S L L A P S
B D G C Y I E O S E E K T E N I L T
U E U R A P E R I I C G T O I E E I
I R E T P R E T E O D H A A E S X C
I E P I R T T T R U D N D I H S M W
F A L S A S W E D I S H T I L E S A
C C T W D S H U O E E R N E S U R F
O R T T P T I D A O N D R T T U E R
```

Look for these words:

CONVICTS

LANDMARK

SYDNEYSIDER

THE ROCKS

FUTURISTIC

COLONY

SWEDISH TILES

NEW SOUTH WALES

WATERSKIING

CLIPPER SHIP

SURF

AUSTRALIA

BUBONIC PLAGUE

ARTS COMPLEX

CAPTAIN PHILLIP

GALLERIES

SAILING

Tokyo, Japan

Tokyo is located on the southern shore of the island of Honshu. It is on Japan's largest area of flat land, surrounded on three sides by mountains. Fujiyama, Japan's highest peak, can be seen from the city center. Tokyo began as a small fishing village about 400 years ago, when the warrior Ieyasu Tokugawa built the famous Edo Castle on the **site**. At that time, the city was called Edo. All that is left today of Edo Castle is the stone **foundation** which lies on the grounds of the Imperial Castle where the Emperor of Japan lives. It is open to visitors only two days each year—on the Emperor's birthday and for Japan's New Year's celebration. There are gardens, art **galleries**, and a theater on the palace grounds. The palace is protected by stone walls and a series of wide **moats**.

Tokyo has many beautiful gardens and parks that are filled with cherry blossoms in the spring. Ueno Park, about 2 miles (3.7 km) from the palace, also has a large concert hall, several museums, art galleries, a zoo, a temple, and a **shrine**. Many of Tokyo's festivals are held in the park and **center** around blooming flowers. The Cherry Blossom Festival is in April when people gather to picnic under the thick, sweet blossoms. There is a Plum Blossom Festival in February and a Chrysanthemum Festival in October.

There are so many people in Tokyo that **competition** for new housing is **fierce**. As soon as construction on a *danchi*, a public apartment, is completed, names are put into a **lottery** to decide who gets the new apartments. Homes are generally very small and are a peaceful **respite** from the **bustling** city. Shoes are always removed when entering a dwelling in Japan, a practical and symbolic **gesture** so as not to bring any of the dirt or **stress** from the outside world into the home.

Tokyo residents enjoy the national sport of Japan, sumo wrestling. They also participate in sports like baseball, golf, ice skating, and tennis. Tokyo's professional baseball team, the Tokyo Giants, plays at Korakuem Stadium.

Answer in complete sentences:

1. What is Japan's highest peak?
2. Who built Edo Castle on the site of Tokyo?
3. For what occasions is the Imperial Palace open to visitors?
4. What attractions are located in Ueno Park?
5. Name Tokyo's professional baseball team.

Web Site:
http://www.jwindow.net/

Language Arts

You will need:

✔ nonfiction information about Japan
✔ encyclopedia volume T (Tokyo)
✔ paper
✔ pencil

Write a description of a typical Japanese home and furnishings. What housing is available in downtown Tokyo?

Research Studies

You will need:

✔ Japanese cookbooks
✔ nonfiction books about Japan
✔ paper
✔ pencil

What are *sushi*, *tempura*, and *sukiyaki*? How is food eaten in traditional Japanese restaurants?

Social Studies

You will need:

✔ nonfiction information about Japan
✔ nonfiction information about typhoons and earthquakes in Japan
✔ paper
✔ pencil

Explain how weather and natural disasters affect life in Tokyo. In what year was Tokyo almost destroyed by an earthquake?

Language Arts

You will need:

✔ nonfiction information about Japan
✔ tourist books about Japan
✔ paper
✔ pencil

Write a description of a Tokyo capsule hotel. Why are they popular? Who uses them? Would you be willing to stay in one?

Tokyo, Japan

Three important Japanese national holidays are:

Adults' Day: January 15
Children's Day: May 5
Respect for the Aged Day: September 15

Choose one holiday and complete two of these projects. Then, design a banner or greeting card for the holiday.

▲ Research the background of the holiday. Write a report to share with the class.
▲ Write a haiku for the holiday.
▲ Explain how the holiday might be observed by a typical Tokyo family.
▲ Write an original story or journal entry telling what happened on the holiday.

Europe

Europe is smaller than every other continent in the world except Australia. It is located on the western side of the world's largest landmass, which includes both Asia and Europe (sometimes called Eurasia). The boundaries of Europe extend from the Arctic Ocean in the north to the Mediterranean Sea in the south, and from the Atlantic Ocean in the west to the Ural Mountains in the east. Europe is divided into 47 countries, including the largest country in the world, Russia, and the smallest, Vatican City. About 713 million people live in Europe.

Beginning with the early Greek and Roman civilizations, Europeans have made important contributions to government, art, and science. The Industrial Revolution (1700) began in Europe and marked the start of manufacturing around the world. Many European countries kept colonies in Africa and Asia in order to have enough raw materials and a market for their manufactured goods.

Europe has areas of natural beauty and fertile farmland. There are mountain ranges and grassy plains. Rivers provide electricity, irrigation, and transportation routes. About one-sixth of the people earn their living through farming. Farmers, helped by mild climates, good rainfall, and modern equipment, produce more crops per acre than anywhere in the world.

Some of the larger and more famous cities of the world are in Europe. London, Paris, and Rome are major cities with cathedrals, palaces, museums, landmarks, and ancient ruins that attract visitors from all parts of the world. The Swiss Alps, French Riviera, Black Forest, and tulip fields of the Netherlands are all part of Europe's natural beauty.

World War I (1914–1918) and World War II (1939–1945) began in Europe. The wars destroyed property and cost many lives. They brought about changes in the governments of many countries. Eastern European countries were ruled by Communists until the end of 1991 when the Soviet Union collapsed.

In 1993, 15 Western European countries formed a group called the European Union. The headquarters for the European Union is in Brussels, Belgium.

Amsterdam, Netherlands

Amsterdam is more than 700 years old. The name means "dam of the Amstel." It is a city of 90 islands divided by canals. Because the entire city is below sea level, the soil is so soft that buildings must be placed on wooden posts so they do not sink. For many years, windmills kept Amsterdam from being flooded. Today, the city uses electrically-powered pumps to move **excess** water out to sea, but some of the old windmills are restored and protected by the government. The windmills are a reminder of the city's historical roots and a symbol of Dutch culture. Amsterdam is a small, **quaint** city with a laid-back atmosphere. The **cobblestone** streets are lined with coffee houses, book stores, and antique shops. The bicycles on Amsterdam's streets outnumber the cars. The old section of the city is completely closed to automobile traffic because the streets are so narrow.

Amsterdam is a city very proud of its artists and painters. The Rijksmuseum is one of the best museums in the world. This simple red brick and wooden building is characteristically Dutch and houses prized paintings and sculptures. The most famous painting is Rembrandt's *Night Watch,* which has an entire room **dedicated** to its **display.** Another famous Dutch painter has an entire museum to house his work. The National Vincent van Gogh Museum has over 200 paintings, 500 drawings, and many letters by the great artist.

Amsterdam's canals make it possible to **access** any part of the city by boat. Water taxis are a popular way to travel. There are many markets, shops, and stores right along the canals. *Bloemenmarkt,* the world's only floating flower market, consists of four blocks of barges in the canal. There are colorful displays of potted plants, bulbs, and freshly cut flowers. Amsterdam's people have a tradition of bringing flowers as gifts when visiting a home for the first time, and for many other occasions.

Answer in complete sentences:

1. What is the meaning of the name Amsterdam?
2. Why are cars prohibited in Amsterdam's city center?
3. Where is the seat of government for the Netherlands?
4. Why is it necessary for the city to have an extensive canal system?
5. What would you find at *Bloemenmarkt?*

Web Sites:

http://www.openworld.co.uk/cityguides/amsterdam/
http://www.channels.nl/adam.html

Language Arts

You will need:
- ✔ pencil
- ✔ paper
- ✔ art supplies

Living on a houseboat is part of daily life for many people in Amsterdam. How would your life be different if you lived in a houseboat on a canal? Write a story and make a drawing or model of a houseboat.

Social Studies

You will need:
- ✔ nonfiction books about Amsterdam and the Netherlands
- ✔ paper
- ✔ pencil

Make a list of products that are exported from the Netherlands. Which ones are used by your family?

Art/History

You will need:
- ✔ nonfiction information about Rembrandt and his paintings
- ✔ paper
- ✔ pencil

The Rembrandt House in Amsterdam was restored after World War II. Write a brief biography of the painter. Describe one of his paintings. Explain his use of light and shadow and how he shows action in his portraits.

Art

You will need:
- ✔ pictures of work by Vincent van Gogh
- ✔ orange and yellow tissue paper
- ✔ scissors
- ✔ glue stick
- ✔ markers
- ✔ white drawing paper

Use the art supplies to make a picture of sunflowers with tissue paper petals.

Anne Frank House

Located in the heart of Amsterdam, this house is a world-famous museum where a young Jewish girl and her family hid from the Nazis during World War II. The cramped quarters, called The Annex, were shared by four members of the Frank family and four of their acquaintances. A visitor can see the rooms where they lived and read excerpts from Anne's diary.

The group was in isolation from July 8, 1942, until August 4, 1944, when the Germans found them. They were sent to concentration camps. Anne got typhus and died at age 15, just 2 months before the British liberated the camp. She wrote in her diary, "I want to go on living even after my death."

After reading an excerpt from the beginning of Anne's diary, answer these questions.

1. Explain the location of the Annex. _____

   _____

   _____

2. Why did the family have to go into hiding? _____

   _____

   _____

3. When did Anne receive her diary? What did she call her diary? _____

   _____

   _____

4. Name the four members of the Frank family. _____

   _____

   _____

5. How did the family get food and provisions? _____

   _____

   _____

6. What did the people in hiding do to pass time during the day? _____

   _____

   _____

Athens, Greece

Athens is the site of two cities. The modern Athens is built on top of and **amid** the great ancient civilization. The large flat hill called the Acropolis was the center of original Athenian life. It was the birthplace of **democracy** and Western **philosophy**. Temples and government buildings with grand **arcades** of **columns** and marble statues line the Acropolis. Many of the **frescoes** and **friezes** that decorated the temples have been moved to a nearby museum to protect then from the damaging industrial pollution of modern Athens. The most magnificent temple on the Acropolis is called the Parthenon, dedicated to the goddess Athena. Most of the Acropolis is still standing.

Below the Acropolis is a charming neighborhood called *Plaka*. It has been restored to its original condition. The apartments are painted in colorful **pastels** and have **wrought iron** balconies with bright geraniums in the flower boxes. Some of the streets in *Plaka* are so narrow that only one person can pass at a time. The area is dotted with souvenir shops, **taverns**, and small churches.

In Greece, the food is simple and elegant, much like Greek art and architecture. In the many *tavernas* (cafes) in Athens, traditional Greek food is served on patios lined with olive trees. An Athenian meal might include stuffed grape leaves and grilled lamb.

Near the Acropolis is the Theater of Dionysus which seated 15,000 **spectators**. This was the site of many original Greek dramatic performances. Greece's largest temple is the Temple of Olympian Zeus and is near the theater. The Roman Agora, also in the area, is an ancient marketplace covered with a **colonnade**. Today, it is still a market where street vendors sell lace cloth and **embroidery**. In ancient Greece, the Agora was not only a market, but a daily meeting place for hearing news and discussing politics.

Answer in complete sentences:

1. Where is Athens located?
2. What is Greece's largest temple called?
3. Where is the Parthenon? Whom does it honor?
4. Describe the neighborhood of *Plaka*.
5. What do street vendors sell in the Agora?

Web Sites:
http://www.mechan.ntua.gr/webacropol/
http://www.dilos.com/region/attica/athens.html

Research

You will need:
- ✔ encyclopedia volume G
- ✔ paper
- ✔ pencil

Make a chart of famous Greeks in these categories: writers, philosophers, poets. List one work for each of them.

Language Arts

You will need:
- ✔ tourist brochures
- ✔ paper
- ✔ pencil

Athens is a tourist city. Read the information and estimate the cost of plane fare and three nights in an Athens hotel.

Art

You will need:
- ✔ encyclopedia volume C (columns)
- ✔ paper
- ✔ pencil

Copy drawings of the Doric, Ionian, and Corinthian columns. Describe the similarities and differences among the styles.

Social Studies

You will need:
- ✔ Mediterranean or Greek cookbook
- ✔ paper
- ✔ pencil

Find a recipe that uses feta cheese. Prepare a snack of feta and crackers to share with the class.

Athens, Greece
Crossword Puzzle

ACROSS

2. Product sold by street vendors in the Agora
5. Temple dedicated to Athena
6. Charming neighborhood in Athens
11. Statues at the Acropolis were made out of ___.
12. Birthplace of democracy
13. Greek cafe
14. Kind of balcony railing
15. Hill where the Parthenon is located

DOWN

1. Olives grow on ___.
3. In ancient Greece, a subject to discuss at the Agora
4. What covers the Agora
7. Marketplace in Athens
8. Kind of meat grilled in Athens
9. Goddess whom the Parthenon honors
10. Kind of flowers seen in Plaka

Barcelona, Spain

Barcelona lies on the Mediterranean Sea between two mountain peaks. It is in the region of Spain called Catalonia, home to the **fiercely** independent and political Catalan people. The city is a cultural and economic center and a beautiful city with much history and an exciting future.

Barcelona has two **distinct** sections. The modern *El Eixample* and the medieval Gothic Quarter. The old city was surrounded with stone walls until 1860 when the walls came down. This allowed the city to grow. Out of it rose the elegant *Eixample* area with wide tree-lined avenues, gardens, and **luxurious** homes. The fashionable streets were home to **trend-setting** architects who designed many unusual buildings. One apartment building has a huge stone front with balconies that look like waves **rippling** around the block. Another building, an art gallery, has a tangled metal sculpture that looks like hair sticking out from the top of it.

The Gothic Quarter has many reminders of the Roman occupation. The narrow streets are **prohibited** to cars and wind past buildings built thousands of years ago. There are antique and **flea markets**, cafes, and galleries, including the Picasso Museum which is housed in two 15th-century palaces.

The city's best known landmark is Sagrada Familia, a cathedral built by the famous architect Antoni Gaudí. Gaudí died in 1926 leaving no plans for the immense building. It is still under construction. Its future is unknown because of **intense controversy** over the cathedral's sculptures, one of which shows Christ in the nude. When completed, Sagrada Familia will be Europe's largest cathedral with a dome over 500 feet (152 m) high.

Answer in complete sentences:

1. Who founded the city of Barcelona?
2. When were the walls of the old city taken down?
3. What is Sagrada Familia? What is unusual about the structure?
4. Where is the Picasso Museum located?
5. What are the two sections of Barcelona?

Web Site:
http://city.net/countries/spain/barcelona

Geography

You will need:
- ✔ encyclopedia volume S
- ✔ drawing paper
- ✔ colored pencils

Draw a map of Spain, labeling the Catalonia region, the Pyrenees Mountains, Barcelona, and Madrid.

Research

You will need:
- ✔ nonfiction information about European cathedrals, particularly Sagrada Familia
- ✔ paper
- ✔ pencil

Explain the construction style of the Sagrada Familia. What does a visitor see? Write at least three reasons why the building is not yet complete.

Social Studies

You will need:
- ✔ nonfiction books about Christopher Columbus
- ✔ world map
- ✔ paper

Explain Christopher Columbus's connection to Barcelona. Name his ships and trace his route from Spain to the New World.

Art

You will need:
- ✔ art history books on Picasso
- ✔ art supplies

Make a drawing or collage in one of Picasso's styles. Label the style.

Barcelona, Spain

Research information about the 1992 Barcelona Summer Olympics. List five events and name the medal-winning athletes.

1. _____
   (event)

   gold_____

   silver_____

   bronze _____

2. _____
   (event)

   gold_____

   silver_____

   bronze _____

3. _____
   (event)

   gold_____

   silver_____

   bronze _____

4. _____
   (event)

   gold _____

   silver_____

   bronze _____

5. _____
   (event)

   gold _____

   silver_____

   bronze _____

Berlin, Germany

Berlin began as a trading village on the northeast bank of the Spree River. Throughout history, Berlin has **prospered** as a center for trade, business, science, and culture. It has also suffered the destruction of two world wars. After Germany lost World War II, the city was divided into two sections. East Berlin was governed by the Communists and West Berlin remained non-communist.

The Berlin Wall was built to keep people in the East from leaving. For 28 years, the wall of concrete and barbed wire was guarded 24 hours a day. Movement between the two sections of the city was greatly **restricted**. In 1989, the wall came down when the non-communists won control of the entire city. Today, one can still see parts of the crumbling wall. You can even buy a piece of the famous wall, which was made of concrete mixed with small rocks. However, many **swindlers** have taken to making their own wall pieces and selling them to unsuspecting tourists.

The oldest section of the city, called *Mitte* (center), was the business and cultural center of East Berlin. The German government is working to improve conditions and **update** the East to match the modern **conveniences** in the West and make a united Berlin.

Checkpoint Charlie was the main entrance leading in or out of East Berlin during the Cold War. There is a museum there, today, which **depicts** the many ways in which East Berliners attempted to escape to West Berlin. In one case, the escapees dug a hole under the wall, but they made sure that the tunnel was big enough so their wives could walk to freedom, not crawl.

Answer in complete sentences:

1. How was Berlin affected by Germany's loss of World War II?
2. What was the purpose of the Berlin Wall? When was it built? How long did it stand?
3. What is the *Mitte*?
4. What was the name of the main entrance between the two sections of Berlin?
5. What are two ways that East Berliners attempted to escape from West Berlin?

Web Sites:
http://www.chemie.fu-berlin.de/adressen/berlin.html

Research

You will need:
- ✔ nonfiction historical information about the Olympics
- ✔ paper
- ✔ pencil

What medals were won by Jesse Owens at the 1936 Olympics? Why did his success represent a problem for Adolf Hitler and the Nazis?

Social Studies

You will need:
- ✔ travel books and brochures for Berlin
- ✔ paper
- ✔ pencil

Write a three-day travel itinerary to Berlin for your family. Explain why you have chosen certain sites for specific family members. Decide on a month for your trip and research the weather conditions. Make a packing list of appropriate clothing.

Language Arts

You will need:
- ✔ German/English dictionary
- ✔ paper
- ✔ pencil

Choose one project to write in the German language:
- ▲ a typical lunch or dinner menu
- ▲ the numbers 1–10
- ▲ the primary colors
- ▲ a list of school supplies
- ▲ a pictionary with six clothing items

Art/Music

You will need:
- ✔ encyclopedia volume B
- ✔ map of Germany
- ✔ paper
- ✔ pencil

Read the biographies of Johann Sebastian Bach and Ludwig van Beethoven. Locate the German cities where each composer lived, worked, and performed. Make lists of events from their lives that occurred in Berlin.

Berlin Wall

Use reference materials or the Internet to answer these questions about the Berlin Wall.

1. What political events led to the construction of the wall? _____

   _____

   _____

2. What German leader ordered the building of the wall? _____

   When did construction begin? _____

3. Explain why the Western allies did not react harshly to the building of the wall.

   _____

   _____

   _____

4. Describe the completed wall and the system of barriers. _____

   _____

   _____

   _____

5. What events led to the removal of the wall? _____

   _____

   _____

6. Name the political leaders in West Germany, East Germany, the United States, and the Soviet Union at the time the Berlin Wall came down.

   West Germany _____   United States _____

   East Germany _____   Soviet Union _____

7. What is the Brandenburg Gate? What is Checkpoint Charlie? _____

   _____

Budapest, Hungary

The Danube River splits the city of Budapest into two sections—Buda and Pest. Nazis destroyed 33,000 of the city's buildings and all of its 8 connecting bridges during World War II. The Soviet Union occupied Budapest until 1956. The public buildings have been **reconstructed** to look like the **originals.** This capital city remains the cultural and industrial center of Hungary.

Pest is where most of the city's people live. It is modern with glass and steel buildings. Hotels, apartment **complexes**, and lovely parks line the Danube. Budapest is a city **obsessed** with statues and sculpture. There are more than 500 statues all over the squares, public buildings, and churches. Statue Park was created outside the city to keep statues of the old Soviet political figures.

The oldest part of the city, called Buda, is full of rolling hills covered with historic homes, some of which still have bullet holes from the war. There are many charming **pastel** houses, the colors of which used to **signify** the **trade** of the owner. The historic Chain Bridge crosses into Castle Hill in Buda where artists, writers, and students gather along the narrow, winding streets at coffee shops, book stores, and libraries. There is a special Youth Park near Castle Hill that is used for teenage dances and rock concerts.

Margaret Island is **situated** in the middle of the Danube River between Pest and Buda. It is a beautiful recreational area with lakes, a rose garden, a sports arena, and more than 10,000 trees. In the summer, there are outdoor concerts, plays, and films.

Answer in complete sentences:

1. Where do most people live in Budapest?
2. Describe the older part of Budapest.
3. What kinds of people spend time in Castle Hill?
4. How was the city affected by the Nazis during World War II?
5. Why do you think the Soviet statues were moved to their own park?

Web Sites:
http://www.budapest.com/
http://city.net/countries/hungary/budapest/

Geography

You will need:

✔ nonfiction books about European rivers and trade routes and encyclopedia volume D
✔ paper
✔ pencil

Explain the Danube's importance as a trade route for the countries of eastern and central Europe. What other port cities are on the Danube?

Research

You will need:

✔ international cookbooks
✔ paper
✔ pencil

Locate and write a recipe for Hungarian goulash. What spices are traditional in Hungarian homes? What foods are common?

Music

You will need:

✔ biography of Bartók and encyclopedia volume B
✔ paper
✔ pencil
✔ recordings

Write a brief biography of Béla Bartók. Make a list of five of his most famous works. Listen to a recording.

Social Studies

You will need:

✔ nonfiction information about Hungary
✔ paper
✔ pencil

Explain how life in Budapest has changed since the people overthrew the communist regime. How was the transition made to a democratic form of government? What is the current status of the economy? Explain the organization of government.

Budapest, Hungary

Word Search Puzzle

```
S B N E N H S M E T I H D W E H E P
A R H E D E U S W R E E R A E W S J
T C E E A N E N R E I S C R I T M N
L O W U N A T T G P U L H E R E A A
N F L T U S S H U A E L A E T T R D
A F O D B A N C E T R H I R E A G E
A E T H E E C H H J M Y N S N L A E
R E E Y R O H Y W D T N B N F I R L
N S N E I E S B L F E A R R N O E E
O H N W V E E E E D T Z I A C B T C
B O E H E A N R Y U U I D E N U I B
E P T C R L U A A O A S G A P D S R
E O C A S T L E H I L L E H T A L P
A I N E P O M P E S T E E W I E A T
E I E L H I S T O R I C H E U U N X
R E U B R I D G E S T E S O R I D O
O C P E T T G T I P H R E R C C E O
S T A T U E P A R K E I S D E E N A
```

Look for these words:

DANUBE RIVER

PEST

CHAIN BRIDGE

MARGARET ISLAND

HUNGARY

SCULPTURE

OCCUPIED

WAR

BUDA

STATUE PARK

CASTLE HILL

COFFEE SHOP

BRIDGES

HISTORIC

NAZIS

Edinburgh, Scotland

The city of Edinburgh is **dominated** by the dramatic Edinburgh Castle **perched** on top of Castle Rock. Some of Napoleon's soldiers were held in Edinburgh Castle. There are still carvings by the Frenchmen on the prison **vault's** walls. Near the entrance to the castle is the **daunting** Witches Well, the site of 300 witch burnings. From the castle, the Royal Mile leads down **craggy** cliffs and steep mountains, past narrow alleys and princely estates. It ends at the Palace of Holyroodhouse, the residence of Queen Elizabeth when she is in Scotland.

Princes Street, Queen Street, and George Street make up the New Town district. They run **parallel** to each other with a square at each end. The buildings in this section were built in the 18th century and house elegant stores and restaurants. On George Street, one can find many quaint boutiques where Scottish **tartans** and woolens are sold.

Edinburgh is often called a golfer's paradise. The city runs six golf courses surrounded by rocky coast and countryside. It is believed that Mary, Queen of Scots enjoyed golf on Edinburgh's Bruntsfield Links, one of the oldest courses in the world.

Edinburgh's International Festival is held in August and attracts people from around the world. The city becomes a world stage for dramatic and musical productions, usually accompanied by a major art **exhibition**. The festival began as a way to bring back the **vitality** and joy of life for Scotland's citizens after World War II.

Answer in complete sentences:

1. For whom is the city of Edinburgh named?
2. Who lives in the Palace at Holyroodhouse?
3. Name the three streets in the New Town district.
4. What could a tourist see at Edinburgh Castle?
5. What is a popular sport in Scotland?

Web Sites:
http://www.uktravel.com/uk/scotland.html
http://www.edinburgh.org/

Research

You will need:
- ✔ international cookbooks
- ✔ paper
- ✔ pencil

From what is *haggis* made? Read a recipe. Would you be willing to sample this traditional Scottish food? Explain.

Language Arts

You will need:
- ✔ dictionary
- ✔ nonfiction information about castles and palaces
- ✔ paper
- ✔ pencil

Design a pictionary showing 10 terms relating to castles and palaces.

Social Studies/Geography

You will need:
- ✔ nonfiction information about sports
- ✔ paper
- ✔ pencil

Golf is a popular sport in Scotland. There are 28 golf courses within the city boundaries of Edinburgh. What equipment is necessary for golf? Explain the rules and how to score a game.

Art/Research

You will need:
- ✔ nonfiction information about Scotland
- ✔ paper
- ✔ crayons or markers

Locate and draw three Scottish clan tartans. Explain the practice of assigning a special plaid to clans or family groups.

Edinburgh, Scotland

The Palace of Holyroodhouse and Edinburgh Castle are on opposite ends of the Royal Mile. They are important Edinburgh landmarks.

Read these sentences. Decide if the sentence is describing the palace or the castle. Answer PHH (Palace of Holyroodhouse), EC (Edinburgh Castle), or BOTH.

1. The Scottish home of the British royal family _____

2. Tourists enjoy visiting the structure. _____

3. It is built on a hill overlooking the city. _____

4. Visitors enter through a gatehouse. _____

5. Ruins of the Abbey Church are on the grounds. _____

6. The oldest building is St. Margaret's Chapel. _____

7. The complex was originally built as a fortress. _____

8. There is a palace on the grounds. _____

9. Beautiful paintings and tapestries decorate the walls. _____

10. Visitors can see the crown jewels and armor. _____

11. The one o'clock gun is fired from the battery every day. _____

12. Fine furniture is displayed in the royal apartments. _____

Istanbul, Turkey

Istanbul is **unique** in many ways. For example, it is the only major city in the world that lies in two continents, Europe and Asia. It has been known by three different names—Byzantium, Constantinople, and now, Istanbul. It has been the capital city of the Roman, Byzantine, and Ottoman Empires. Today, it is not a capital city for the first time in 16 centuries.

The three empires have left Istanbul with some of the world's most **impressive** structures, such as Islamic mosques, Greek temples, and Roman cathedrals. When the Hagia Sophia, a Byzantine church, was built, it was so amazingly huge inside that people were afraid to enter it for fear it would collapse. The Blue Mosque is named for the beautiful blue tile work lining the inside walls that makes delicate floral patterns of lilies, tulips, and roses. The mosque has six tall **minarets**, instead of the usual four.

Topkapi Palace is now a museum that exhibits treasures of the Ottoman sultans. Jewelry, art, furnishings, and some of the world's biggest diamonds and emeralds are on display. The palace has four courtyards, ten kitchens, and beautiful **rococo** fountains that the sultan would order turned on so that servants could not overhear his conversations.

The Golden Horn is an **inlet** of the Bosporus Strait that divides the European side of Istanbul into old and new sections. The old section has narrow cobblestone streets, parks, and mosques. Also in this area is Istanbul's Grand Bazaar where carpets, gold, leather, pipes, **fezzes**, and countless other items are sold. It features over 4,000 shops in a covered open-air building with high ceilings, tiled walls, and **pillars**.

Answer in complete sentences:

1. What other names has Istanbul had throughout history?
2. How does the Golden Horn divide the city?
3. Explain Istanbul's location on two continents.
4. What can a tourist see at the Topkapi Palace?
5. What is the Hagia Sophia?

Web Site:
http://www.city.net/countries/turkey/istanbul/

Art

You will need:
- ✔ nonfiction information about Turkey and Islam
- ✔ paper
- ✔ pencil
- ✔ art supplies

Research the Muslim style of dress for men and women. How is it different in the cities than in rural areas? Draw pictures of both men and woman in the cities and in the country.

Research

You will need:
- ✔ paper
- ✔ pencil

What is meant by the term "melting pot"? Do research to explain how Istanbul is a melting pot for the races and religions of Europe and Asia.

Social Studies

You will need:
- ✔ nonfiction information about Turkey and Islam
- ✔ paper
- ✔ pencil

How does the Muslim religion influence the traditions and culture of Turkey? How are tourists affected by Islam when they visit Istanbul?

Social Studies

You will need:
- ✔ international cookbooks
- ✔ paper
- ✔ pencil

Read recipes for Turkish foods that use lamb, rice, eggplant, or vegetables stuffed in cabbage leaves. Select a main dish and write a shopping list for dinner for four. What would a Turkish family probably drink with dinner?

Istanbul, Turkey

Label these landmarks in Central Istanbul. Then label the Golden Horn, the Bosphorus, and the Sea of Marmara.

1. Ayasofya Museum_____   3. Blue Mosque_____

2. Covered Bazaar _____   4. Topkapi Palace _____

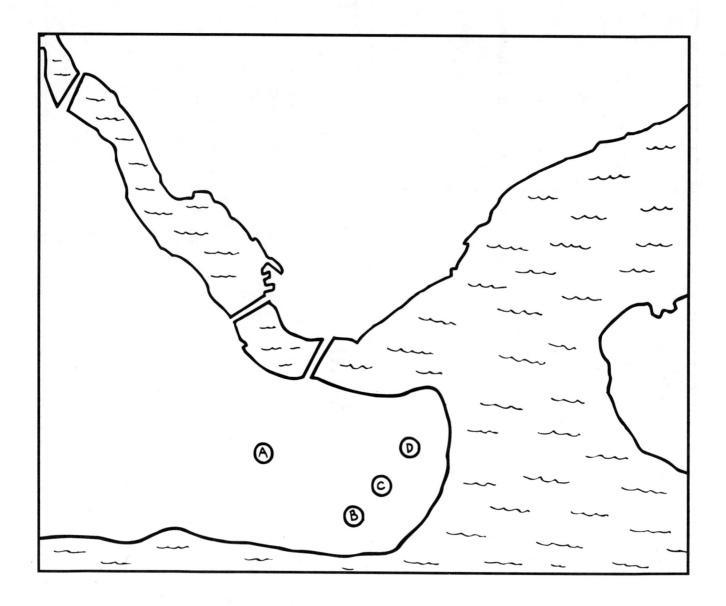

Kiev, Ukraine

Kiev is the capital of Ukraine, a country in Eastern Europe that is about the size of Texas. The Ukrainian people have been **oppressed** and Kiev has been destroyed many times; by the Germans, Russians, Poles, and Lithuanians. In 1986, the **nuclear reactor** in Chernobyl, only 80 miles (130 km) from Kiev, exploded. The beautiful Dnieper River that runs through the city is no longer safe for swimming and it is said that its **silt** bottom is **radioactive**. In spite of these **setbacks**, Ukraine is now enjoying its freedom and restoring the buildings,

monuments, and museums important to Ukrainian culture. The city remains a quaint, quiet place **teeming** with history and pride.

One of the national heroes, who has a university, museum, square, and monument dedicated to him in Kiev, **signifies** the city's pride. Taras Shevchenko was a poet, artist, and political **activist** who fought for Ukraine's freedom. He was born a serf (slave) under Russian rule but was freed by his owner in appreciation of his artistic talents. Shevchenko was thrown in prison by the Russians because of his work that told the sad tale of Russian **oppression** against his people. Shevchenko's work can be viewed at the Shevchenko State Museum.

St. Sophia's Cathedral is **modeled** after Hagia Sophia in Istanbul, but with Ukrainian woodworking techniques. Throughout history, the cathedral has been bombed, burned, and **defaced**. Many times, it has been restored and changed to fit the ruling culture. There are 9 golden domes and a 250-foot (76-m) bell tower topping the structure. The **mosaic** work inside is especially grand with 25 tons of gold and silver in the tiles. On the cathedral grounds is the Monastery of the Caves. These deep **caverns** were originally used by monks to hide from invaders back in the 11th century. The caves contain over 40 tombs and a maze of **catacombs** that connect to a series of other churches and cathedrals.

Answer in complete sentences:

1. What is a serf?
2. What countries ruled Kiev?
3. What outside factors have damaged Kiev over the years?
4. What can a visitor see at the Monastery of the Caves?
5. What river runs through Kiev?

Web Site:
http://www.omg.unb.ca/~ipad/kiev.html

Research

You will need:

➤ nonfiction information about Ukraine

➤ crayons or markers

➤ paper

➤ pencil

Explain the two methods of Ukrainian egg decoration, *krashanka* and *pysanka*. Draw an example of each one. What do Ukrainians believe about the power of eggs?

Social Studies

You will need:

➤ nonfiction information about Ukraine and Chernobyl

➤ paper

➤ pencil

How was Kiev affected by the nuclear explosion at Chernobyl? Where is Chernobyl located in relation to Kiev?

Geography

You will need:

➤ map of the world

➤ pencil

➤ paper

Trace the route from your hometown to Kiev. What countries and bodies of water would you fly over?

Art

You will need:

➤ art history books

➤ paper

➤ pencil

Explain the techniques of fresco and mosaic. What supplies were used to produce each type of artwork?

Chernobyl

In April of 1986, there was an explosion of a reactor at the Chernobyl nuclear plant. The blast threw nine tons of radioactive particles into the air. When high doses of radioactive materials strike living tissue, they cause cancer, birth defects, or death.

Choose one of the following:

1. Research the importance of nuclear energy in Ukraine.

2. Research and explain the present-day condition of Chernobyl.

3. Research the long-term effects of radiation exposure.

4. Locate Chernobyl and Stockholm, Sweden, on a map of the world. Using that distance as a radius, draw a circle. List the locations that fall within the circle. These cities/countries were also affected by the radiation fallout.

Discussion Topic:

Soviet leader Mikhail Gorbachev announced the explosion to the people of the Soviet Union two days after it happened because Swedish scientists detected high levels of radiation passing over Sweden. Valuable time was lost in evacuating people and destroying dangerous animals and crops. Because of the delay, thousands of people were exposed to deadly levels of radiation.

How was Mikhail Gorbachev's announcement about the Chernobyl explosion influenced by the Cold War? How were the people of Kiev affected by the delayed announcement? Would this situation be handled differently if it happened in Ukraine today? Explain.

_____

_____

_____

_____

_____

_____

_____

_____

_____

London, England

Big Ben Clock Tower, Westminster Abbey, Parliament, the Tower of London, and St. Paul's Cathedral—these are all famous landmarks located in one great city, London, England. London began as a small Roman village along the Thames River. Farm animals roamed the narrow, cobblestone streets of 14th-century London. The Thames was polluted with garbage. **Contagious** diseases were **rampant**. The houses were made of wood and heated with coal, so fires were common and **devastating**. Despite these difficult conditions, London quickly developed into a busy trade and finance center.

Many kings and queens have ruled England and lived in London. One of the most famous was Queen Victoria who became queen at age 18. During her **reign**, the British Empire became an important world power, including one-quarter of the world's people. Although there is no longer a British Empire, London is a **vital** city with a rich past.

London is the largest city in Europe and has some of the finest galleries, museums, restaurants, department stores, and theaters. The Tate Gallery has a massive collection of 19th- and 20th-century art, including an entire wing dedicated to J. M. W. Turner treasures. It would take three or four days to explore the British Museum's **monumental** collection. Harrod's is one of the most famous department stores in the world with plush carpeted aisles and gourmet cafes.

London has beautiful green parks amid its crowded streets. Hyde Park used to be Henry VIII's hunting ground; later it was opened to the public as long as visitors were "properly dressed." London is a city full of things to see and do. Samuel Johnson, a 17th-century writer, said, "If you are tired of London, you are tired of life."

Answer in complete sentences:

1. Name five famous London landmarks.
2. What can you see at the Tate Gallery?
3. Who is the current Queen of England?
4. How old was Queen Victoria when she became queen?
5. Who is Joseph Turner?

Web Sites:
http://www.cineworld.com/Main/main_screen.html
http://www.uktravel.com/london.html

Research

You will need:

✔ encyclopedia volumes and biographies
✔ paper
✔ pencil

Research the contributions of two of these men: William Shakespeare, Charles Dickens, Sir Christopher Wren, Sir Winston Churchill, Henry Purcell, or Geoffrey Chaucer. How did they influence London culture during their lifetimes?

Art

You will need:

✔ *The Guinness Book of World Records*
✔ art supplies

Design a museum display for one of the world records that might be seen at the Trocadero Centre, Piccadilly Circus, London.

Social Studies

You will need:

✔ nonfiction information on World War II, the Industrial Revolution, and the British Empire
✔ paper
✔ pencil

What was the quality of life for Londoners during World War II?

Music

You will need:

✔ research books on English classical music
✔ paper
✔ pencil
✔ recordings

Write a program of three or four compositions that might be played by the Royal Philharmonic at a concert in Royal Festival Hall. Listen to a recording of one of the pieces and share your impressions with the class.

Westminster Abbey

Westminster Abbey is a church for worship as well as the site of royal weddings, coronations, tombs of kings and queens, and memorials to famous politicians, musicians, and poets. More than 3 million people visit the 900-year-old abbey each year. These men are memorialized or buried in Westminster Abbey. Use an encyclopedia or other reference books to categorize their names.

- William Shakespeare
- Lewis Carroll
- Winston Churchill
- Orlando Gibbons
- Charles Dickens
- Robert Peel
- George Frederick Handel
- Henry Purcell
- Henry V

Poets/Writers	*Musicians/Composers*	*Royalty/Politicians*
1._____	1._____	1._____
2._____	2._____	2._____
3._____	3._____	3._____

Choose one person to research. Answer these questions:

1. Name _____ Dates_____

2. Where was he born? _____

3. Where did he work? _____

4. (For poets/writers and musicians/composers) List two of his works. _____

_____

(For royalty/politicians) What was his greatest contribution to his country? _____

_____

_____

Extension: Research the history of Westminster Abbey. Over what period of time was the abbey built? By whom was it designed? _____

_____

_____

Madrid, Spain

Madrid, located in the center of Spain, is a small concentrated city. The downtown area is **crammed** between the Royal Palace and Retiro Park which are only about 1 mile (1.6 km) apart. The summers are hot enough to make the government move to San Sebastian on the coast during August. The winters are cool and dry. Winding medieval streets, red-tiled clay roofs, **monumental** museums, and wide *avenidas* are the rich mixture that makes up Madrid.

In the heart of Madrid is the Plaza Mayor surrounded by broad **arches** and **columns**. This square was built in 1620 by Felipe II and has been the location of criminal **executions**, the burning of **heretics,** the **canonization** of saints, royal marriages, and bullfights. Today, it is closed to the busy car traffic that surrounds it and is a nice quiet place to enjoy sidewalk cafes, street musicians, and portrait artists working in the fresh air.

The huge park called the Retiro is to the east of Madrid's center. This **expansive greenery** has formal gardens, fountains, lakes with rentable rowboats, and a puppet theater. On the weekends, the park is filled with street jugglers, gypsy fortune-tellers, and sidewalk painters. In summer, flamenco concerts are held in the park. Flamenco is a traditional dance and music style of Spanish gypsies that **features** forceful beats and classical Spanish guitar-playing.

One of the world's finest art museums, the Prado, is located in Madrid in front of the Retiro. It exhibits more than 2,000 paintings including works by the great Spanish masters. The collection has been gathered by Spanish royalty since the time of Ferdinand and Isabella, who commissioned Columbus's voyage. One of Madrid's tourist attractions, called Museum Mile, begins at the Prado, and contains more **masterpieces** per meter than anywhere else in the world.

Answer in complete sentences:

1. Why is the capital of Spain moved to San Sebastian during August?
2. Where in Spain is Madrid located?
3. What is the Plaza Mayor?
4. What is flamenco?
5. What is the Prado?

Web Sites:

http://www.cyberspain.com/
http://www.city.net/countries/spain/madrid/

Research

You will need:
- ✔ nonfiction books about Spain and bullfighting
- ✔ Internet access (optional)
- ✔ paper
- ✔ pencil

Use http://www.red2000.com/spain.toros.index.html for historical information about bullfighting. Explain how a bullfight is choreographed. If you were visiting Spain, would you attend a bullfight? Explain.

Language Arts

You will need:
- ✔ paper
- ✔ pencil

It is the custom in Spain to close offices and businesses and leave work for three hours in the middle of each day for a siesta because the sun is very hot. Store hours are 9:00 a.m. to 1:00 p.m. and 4:00 p.m to 7:00 p.m. Explain how this practice could be both good and bad from the points of view of a worker and a shopper.

Social Studies

You will need:
- ✔ international cookbooks
- ✔ paper
- ✔ pencil

Read recipes for *paella* and *gazpacho*, popular Spanish foods. Write directions for making *paella*. Prepare some *gazpacho* to share with the class.

Art

You will need:
- ✔ art history books showing Spanish paintings

Locate works by these Spanish artists: Francisco Goya, Diego Velazquez, Pablo Picasso, and Salvador Dali. Choose one painting that you particularly like and write a brief description of it.

Madrid, Spain

The bullfight, or *corrida*, is a popular form of entertainment in Spain. The bullfighting season is from mid-March until October. There are two large bullfighting rings in Madrid. Color this page, then cut apart the puzzle pieces. Mix up the pieces. Put together your *corrida*. **¡Olé!**

Moscow, Russia

Yuri Dolgoruki scoped out a hill along the banks of the Moscow River, an area easy to defend and convenient for trade and travel to other parts of Russia. There he established Moscow. When Ivan the Terrible became the first czar of the new Russian Empire, the Kremlin was built on the site of Yuri's original village.

The Kremlin, at the heart of the city, is the center of Russian government and its most famous landmark. A series of shiny gold **cupolas** and individual bell towers gracefully top the structure. The Savior Tower clock **looms** over Red Square and keeps time for all of Moscow. One of the bell towers was used as a prison and torture chamber because its thick brick walls **muffled** the voices of the helpless victims inside. Just outside its walls is Red Square, the site of military parades and the location of the Russia Hotel, GUM Department Store, Lenin's Tomb, and St. Basil's Cathedral, which is now a museum. This colorful building looks Disney-like with onion-shaped domes, clashing colors, and **gabled** roofs.

Life in Moscow has changed since Russia became independent in 1991. There are job, housing, and food shortages. Air and water pollution threaten the environment. Organized crime and **counterfeit** money have been difficult to control. However, the city continues to be the center of government and cultural life in Russia. The government has developed programs for **promoting** business, opening up markets to foreign products, and creating jobs. The famous Rolling Stones rock band was finally allowed to play at Moscow's Luzhniki Stadium, after having been **banned** by the Russian government for 30 years.

Muscovites enjoy many museums, concert halls, libraries, and recreational facilities in their city. The Lenin Stadium sports complex includes fields for soccer, track events, and swimming pools. It was built for the 1980 Olympic Games. Gorki Park is another important recreational center that features water sports, ice skating, an outdoor theater, and tennis courts.

Answer in complete sentences:

1. Why did Yuri Dolgoruki locate his village on a hill along the banks of the Moscow River?
2. Who was Vladimir Lenin?
3. Why are the Kremlin and Red Square important to Muscovites?
4. What can a visitor to Gorki Park do for fun?
5. What problems face the local governments of Moscow?

Web Site:
http://www.lonelyplanet.com/dest/eur/mos.htm

Language Arts

You will need:
- ✔ encyclopedia volume K and nonfiction books about the Kremlin
- ✔ paper
- ✔ pencil

Write a story about the things a visitor would see inside the Armory Palace at the Kremlin.

Art

You will need:
- ✔ art supplies
- ✔ paper

Design or draw a building in the style of St. Basil's Cathedral with onion domes and colorful painted details.

Music

You will need:
- ✔ recording of *Peter and the Wolf*
- ✔ markers
- ✔ paper
- ✔ pencil

Listen to Sergei Prokofiev's *Peter and the Wolf*. Choose one of the following: retell the story, write a character study, draw a sketch of three instruments, or make a drawing of the setting.

Social Studies

You will need:
- ✔ chess game
- ✔ paper
- ✔ pencil

Chess is a popular game in Moscow. Learn how to play chess. Write the rules and explain the game to your classmates.

Bolshoi Theater Ballet

The Bolshoi Ballet of Moscow is one of two major ballet companies in Russia. The first ballet was performed at the theater in the late 1700s. The Bolshoi dancers are known for their technical skill and dramatic style. They gained international recognition during a world tour in the 1950s. Famous dancers of the Bolshoi Ballet have included Rudolf Nureyev, Mikhail Baryshnikov, and Anna Pavlova.

Ballet is an important art form. The great Russian composer, Peter Ilyich Tchaikovsky, was particularly skilled at writing lyrical melodies for the dance. Some of his most famous ballets are *Swan Lake, The Nutcracker,* and *The Sleeping Beauty.*

Choose one of the following:

▲ Read a short biography of Peter Ilyich Tchaikovsky and make a time line of 10 important events from his life.

▲ Listen to a recording of Tchaikovsky's music. Write or draw your impressions.

▲ Make a picture book telling the story of one of Tchaikovsky's ballets.

▲ Make a diorama showing a scene from one of Tchaikovsky's ballets.

▲ Design a background setting and puppets to act out a ballet. Write a narration.

▲ Design costumes for a ballet.

▲ List five other compositions by Tchaikovsky.

▲ Read a book about ballet technique. Make a dictionary of 10 ballet terms.

▲ Read about the life of Mikhail Baryshnikov. What is his life like now that he lives in the United States?

▲ Learn the stories of *The Firebird* or *Petrouchka,* ballets by another Russian composer, Igor Stravinsky. Choose one and make drawings of the main character(s).

St. Petersburg, Russia

Peter the Great **established** his capital, St. Petersburg, in northwest Russia on the Gulf of Finland. He wanted the city to be close enough to Europe to **benefit** from Europe's advances in science and technology. St. Petersburg has a beautiful blend of European and Russian architecture.

St. Petersburg is on the Neva River, linked to water routes from the Baltic and Caspian Seas. The city is actually cut by 80 river branches and **canals** into 40 islands. For this reason, St. Petersburg has been called the "Venice of the North." Because it is at sea level, St. Petersburg is often flooded. High **humidity** and fog are common. In winter, **severe** winds howl off the Gulf of Finland and cause ice mists. In late June, the city has "white nights." These are times when only a short **twilight** separates sunrise and sunset.

Many important historical buildings are located in the city. The Winter Palace, former home of the **czars,** is one of the most well known. It took over 6,000 **serfs** to build Peter the Great's palace in the bitter winter wind. **Extreme** temperatures inside and outside the palace caused many workers to die. The Hermitage Museum, as well as St. Peter and St. Paul Cathedral, burial place of Peter the Great, is near the center of the city. Peter the Great's Summer Palace is **styled** after the Palace of Versailles, outside Paris, France. Beautiful ponds, walkways, formal gardens, and fountains fill the area which is now a public park. Eighty statues by Russian sculptors stand in the garden.

Children enjoy visiting Lenin Park which includes a zoo, botanical gardens, a **planetarium**, and several movie houses. There are several large sports stadiums. The biggest is Kirov Stadium which can hold 80,000 people. As a cultural center of Europe, St. Petersburg is home to a symphony orchestra, ballet school and theater, art academy, several important museums, and more than 40 colleges.

Answer in complete sentences:

1. How was the location of St. Petersburg planned to benefit Russia?
2. What are "white nights"?
3. Why is St. Petersburg called the "Venice of the North"?
4. What attractions do people enjoy in Lenin Park?
5. What world-famous art museum is located in St. Petersburg?

Web Site:
http://www-koi.travel.spb.ru/

Research

You will need:
- ✔ world atlas
- ✔ encyclopedia
- ✔ paper
- ✔ pencil

Name two other locations near the Arctic Circle that have "white nights." How do you think "white nights" affect people? Make a list of 10 "how to" suggestions to help keep people sleeping and waking on schedule.

Research

You will need:
- ✔ telephone
- ✔ paper
- ✔ pencil

Contact a travel agency for information about flights to St. Petersburg. Report the schedule and costs of travel to the class. Explain how a traveler obtains a visa and a passport. What types of clothing would be appropriate for the current season in St. Petersburg?

Social Studies

You will need:
- ✔ encyclopedia volumes V and S
- ✔ paper
- ✔ pencil

Compare the topography of Venice, Italy, and St. Petersburg. Why is St. Petersburg called the "Venice of the North"? How do canals add to the charm and tourist appeal of a city? Name two other canal cities in Europe.

Art/Music

You will need:
- ✔ encyclopedia volumes R (Russia) and S (Soviet Union)
- ✔ paper
- ✔ pencil

Make a chart with three names of famous Russians in each of these categories: ballet dancers, composers, and artists.

Peter the Great

Use an encyclopedia or reference book to answer these questions about the czar of Russia.

1. When and where was Peter III born?_____

2. Who was Feodor?_____

   Ivan V? _____

   Sophia? _____

3. What events from Peter's early life made him interested in European technology, science, and art?

   _____

   _____

4. What were Peter's policies within Russia concerning . . .

   the church? _____

   _____

   appointing government officials? _____

   _____

   the power of the czar? _____

   _____

5. How did Peter's programs expand industry, culture, and foreign trade in Russia?

   _____

   _____

6. In what ways was life difficult for the Russian people under Peter's rule?

   _____

   _____

7. Explain three ways St. Petersburg is similar to western European capitals.

   _____

   _____

   _____

Paris, France

Paris, the capital city of France, is one of the cultural centers of the world. Its monuments, cathedrals, and museums are world famous as is its **cuisine** and fashion. The Pompidou Center, the Louvre, the Eiffel Tower, and Notre Dame Cathedral **draw** more than 2 million visitors each year. People from around the world **stroll** the Champs-Élysées, a famous shopping boulevard, and view the Arc de Triomphe.

An island in the Seine River called Île de la Cité, was the heart of **medieval** Paris. The city takes its name from a Gallic tribe, the Parisii, who built bridges that join the island to the river banks. The cathedral of Notre Dame was built on the island in the 12th century. It is still an active church with regular **masses**.

The River Seine winds through Paris for 8 miles (12.8 km). The area on the south side of the river is called the Left Bank. It is home to artists, writers, and students. The University of Paris, called the Sorbonne, was **founded** on the Left Bank in the 13th century. On the Left Bank, tourists shop at open-air stalls for used books and antiques and they can watch artists paint street scenes.

To the north of the Seine is the area called the Right Bank. It is the business section of the city with offices, shopping, and small factories. Many of the city's most famous landmarks are in this section. Since the Middle Ages, magnificent public buildings, churches, palaces, and museums have been built in Paris. Some, like the Louvre, are under constant **renovation**.

Answer in complete sentences:

1. What is the name of Paris's most famous shopping street?
2. Would you prefer to live on the Right or Left Bank of the River Seine? Explain.
3. List five Parisian landmarks.
4. What is the Île de la Cité?
5. What is the Sorbonne?

Web Sites:

http://www.paris.org/
http://www.parisdigest.com/

Geography

You will need:
- map of Paris
- plain white drawing paper
- colored pencils

Draw a map of Paris and add icons for these landmarks: Eiffel Tower, Notre Dame, Arc de Triomphe, and the Louvre. Label the Right and Left Banks. Color the Seine River blue.

Language Arts

You will need:
- French/English dictionary
- paper
- pencil

List 10 words from the French language that refer to food or food preparation. Create a shopping list for one French meal of your choice.

Science

You will need:
- nonfiction information about the Eiffel Tower
- paper
- pencil

Write a page summarizing the construction of the Eiffel Tower. Include statistics about its size and building materials.

Art/Music

You will need:
- encyclopedia volume I and nonfiction books on art and music history
- paper
- pencil

Describe the characteristics of impressionist art and music. Why did the movement begin in France? Make a list of impressionist artists and composers. Include titles of their paintings and compositions.

The Musée du Louvre

The Louvre was originally built near the River Seine to act as a fortress in defense of the city. It was used as a palace until 1682 when the royal court was moved to Versailles. During that time, the buildings fell into **disrepair**, but were **restored** by Napoleon III after the French Revolution. A modern glass **pyramid**, standing in the **plaza** in front of the main buildings, serves as the visitors' entrance.

Today, the Louvre is one of the world's largest and most famous art museums with more than 400,000 **catalogued** pieces. There are six departments: Oriental Antiquities, Egyptian Antiquities, Greek and Roman Antiquities, Paintings, Sculptures, and Art Objects. Among the most important **masterpieces** housed in the museum are the *Mona Lisa* and *Venus de Milo*.

What artist painted the *Mona Lisa?* _____

What sculptor created the *Venus de Milo?*_____

Which department of the Louvre would interest you the most? Explain. List five items you would expect to find there.

_____

_____

_____

_____

_____

Do research to find out when the glass pyramid was added to the Louvre and who designed it.

_____

_____

_____

_____

_____

_____

_____

_____

Prague, Czech Republic

Prague lies on both sides of the Vltava River in the center of the Czech Republic. It has been called the "City of a Hundred **Spires**" because of its many Gothic churches. The city is still recovering from communism which was **expelled** in 1989 during the Velvet Revolution. Student protests and marches started the anti-communist revolt that led to the entire city supporting their cause. Prague is now in the process of shedding the drab gray dust of the **regime** and reclaiming its Czech capital. New stores are opening up, buildings are being restored, and the city has the excitement of an unknown future.

Old Town lies on the right bank of the Vltava River. It served as the seat of government for hundreds of years and has many beautiful buildings and monuments, including the Tyn Church and Charles University. The university, the oldest one in central Europe, was established by Charles IV of Bohemia. He was responsible for Prague's "Golden Era" which made the city a cultural and economic center.

Prague Castle is in the New Town on the left bank of the Vltava River. The castle is the official residence of the president. This castle was reconstructed many times throughout history, but its well known Gothic spires and medieval style were another idea of Charles IV's. Miniature models of the landmark castle are sold in souvenir shops and stands all over Prague. One of the most impressive rooms is Vladislav Hall. It has enormous vaulted ceilings tall enough for **mounted** knights to enter and compete in **jousting tournaments**.

Because of housing shortages, low birth rates, and government controls on **immigration**, the number of people living in Prague has not changed much since World War II. It is one of the few European cities that has room to grow and **expand**. It remains a picturesque and richly historical place.

Answer in complete sentences:

1. What did Charles IV do for Prague?
2. What buildings are in the Old Town?
3. What buildings are in the New Town?
4. Where does the president of the Czech Republic live?
5. What factors have controlled the population growth of Prague?

Web Sites:

http://www.praguesite.cz/
http://sunsite.mff.cuni.cz/prague/
http://www.everydayprague.com/

Research

You will need:
- ✔ biography of Vaclav Havel
- ✔ paper
- ✔ pencil

Write a paragraph explaining Havel's life before he became president of the Czech Republic. List 10 events from his term as president.

Language Arts

You will need:
- ✔ nonfiction information about the Czech Republic
- ✔ paper
- ✔ pencil

What do people in Prague do for entertainment? If you went to a cafe for a meal, what traditional dishes might you choose?

Social Studies

You will need:
- ✔ drawing paper
- ✔ colored pencils

Make a sketch map of Prague showing the Vlatava River, and some buildings in the Old and New Towns.

Art

You will need:
- ✔ art supplies
- ✔ paper

Design a nameplate for a house in Prague based on your future career of choice or based on your favorite hobby, sport, or activity.

Prague, Czech Republic

Use an encyclopedia to research events for each year on the time line. Write one sentence explaining an event for each year on the time line.

Answer these questions:

1. How many years of Prague's history are covered by this chart?

_____
_____
_____
_____

2. For how many years did the Hapsburgs rule Prague?

_____
_____
_____
_____
_____

3. When was the New Town area of Prague built?

_____
_____
_____
_____

4. When was the Old Town area of Prague built?

_____
_____
_____
_____

| 1918 |
| 1945–1948 |
| 1968 |
| 1989 |
| 1993 |

Rome, Italy

From its beginning as a simple farming village built on the banks of the Tiber River, Rome became the center of an ancient empire. Since the waters of the Tiber were too polluted to drink, engineers **ingeniously** designed a system of sewers and **aqueducts** to bring clean water to the people. Beautiful public bathhouses became centers of activity that included gardens, libraries, and shops. Walls were **erected** around the city to protect it from invasion. Today, it is a modern city filled with history, culture, and architecture unequaled anywhere in the world.

The most important industry in Rome today is tourism. The city has carefully **preserved** its ruins, historic buildings, monuments, and fountains in order to **attract** visitors. The Roman Forum, Colosseum, Arch of Constantine, Spanish Steps, Trevi Fountain, and the Pantheon are only a few of the more important landmarks. Restaurants and hotels offer the finest **accommodations** and food service to visitors as Rome is one of the world's most popular **destinations**.

Inside Rome is the Vatican City, a small independent state ruled by the pope. This walled city is the headquarters of the Catholic Church and the location of St. Peter's Basilica, the largest **basilica** in the world and home to the pope. The Vatican Museums and the Sistine Chapel are also in this small city. The Vatican is completely **self-sufficient** with its own post office, bank, radio station, railroad station, and market.

Answer in complete sentences:

1. Why were the aqueducts built?
2. On what river is Rome built?
3. Name five Roman tourist attractions.
4. Explain the structure of Vatican City.
5. Who is the pope?

Web Sites:

http://www.romeguide.it/
http://www.lonelyplanet.com/dest/eur/rom.htm

Research

You will need:

✔ encyclopedia volume R (Rome) and C (catacombs)
✔ paper
✔ pencil

What is the significance of the Roman Catacombs?

Research

You will need:

✔ encyclopedia volume V and nonfiction books on Vatican City
✔ paper
✔ pencil
✔ art supplies

Make a book about Vatican City, its landmarks, and its historical significance to the Catholic church. Explain why it is unique as the smallest independent state in the world.

Language Arts

You will need:

✔ paper
✔ pencil

Use what you know about Rome to explain these sayings: "Rome wasn't built in a day" and "When in Rome, do as the Romans do."

Social Studies

You will need:

✔ Italian/English dictionary
✔ paper
✔ pencil

Brainstorm a list of Italian words that influence our culture. Make a list of 20 words you would need to understand as a tourist in Rome.

Ancient Rome

Ancient Roman society was divided into two groups: the patricians and the plebians. Use reference materials to explain daily activities and family life characteristics of each group.

Patricians

_____

_____

_____

Plebians

_____

_____

_____

Early Romans were the first to recognize the need for local governments. Their laws provide the basis for much of Western legal systems, today. Use reference materials to explain how the Romans influenced the development of law in Europe and in your country.

The Code of Justinian

_____

_____

_____

The Laws of Twelve Tables

_____

_____

_____

Stockholm, Sweden

Stockholm is built on 14 islands and on part of the mainland of Sweden. Bridges connect the sections of the city that are divided by canals. Stockholm is part of a larger **archipelago** of about 24,000 islands, islets, and rocks. Close to the mainland, the islands are larger and the channels are wider. People live on some of these islands. As you go further out to sea, the scenery becomes more **rugged** and the islands are much smaller. Most of these islands are **uninhabited**. Stockholm is a peaceful and quiet city with water-side walkways and medieval streets twisting among the shiny glass and steel high-rise buildings downtown.

The Royal Palace, Parliament, and the Great Church, Stockholm's oldest building, are in Stockholm's Old Town. The main business and shopping district is north of the palace. The *Kulturhuset* (Cultural Center), with art exhibits and stages for theatre, music, and dance performances, is a favorite spot for visitors and Swedish citizens alike. The world's oldest open-air museum, *Skansen,* displays examples of traditional Swedish architecture, including barns, farmhouses, windmills, glassblowing huts, and churches. *Skansen* also has a zoo, a children's circus, and an aquarium. *Globen,* the Stockholm Globe Arena, is the biggest **spherical** building in the world for soccer, ice hockey, and musical events.

In 1998, Stockholm was **honored** as the "Capital of Culture" in Europe. Because of its beauty, cleanliness, and **diverse** cultural life, Stockholm was chosen to host this huge event. There are 70 stages in the city for dance, theatre, and opera productions and 60 museums and art galleries.

Answer in complete sentences:

1. Where is Stockholm located?
2. How do the islands of the archipelago change as you move farther from the mainland?
3. Which would you most like to visit—*Kulturhuset, Skansen,* or *Globen?* Explain your answer.
4. What special honor was given Stockholm in 1998?
5. What is Stockholm's oldest building?

Web Sites:
http://www.stoinfo.se/england/
http://city.net/countries/sweden/stockholm/

Geography

You will need:
- ✔ encyclopedia volume A and a dictionary
- ✔ paper
- ✔ pencil

What is an archipelago? Name two other cities of the world that are built on a group of islands.

Social Studies

You will need:
- ✔ nonfiction books about Sweden
- ✔ paper
- ✔ pencil

Who is the current monarch of Sweden? Draw a diagram that explains the structure of the Swedish government.

Language Arts

You will need:
- ✔ nonfiction information about Sweden
- ✔ paper
- ✔ pencil

What do Swedish children do on Saint Lucia Day?

Art

You will need:
- ✔ large drawing paper
- ✔ markers
- ✔ pencil
- ✔ ruler (optional)

Design a poster advertising Stockholm as the cultural capital of Europe for the year 1998.

Stockholm, Sweden

Word Search Puzzle

```
A W A A D O T R E S C H G A C T O W
A I A P R T E G M O F O C S T T P A
M N N S A C E I R A E G A T N I F L
I D A A N R H E H E I A L B I P E K
P M R O H S L I D R A N D O D F A W
E I T E A O T I P I N T L T B A M A
I L B T E D D S A E I N C A R E N Y
S L C I H O I E D M L R R H N W N S
L E S G I F U E S M E A A R U D N N
E I T E N A W U O N E N G A D R A R
T S O I V S X C E H O D T O R A C E
S L C G L A S S B L O W I N G A N H
E A K E H R N H E E V I A E M O O A
A N H R E A B R I D G E S N V T E B
T D O I K E C R E M T T A G I A H C
N S L S I I O D U R E C A N A L L T
S E M B H G K U L T U R H U S E T E
C I S P H E R I C A L N O A T H O C
```

Look for these words:

ISLANDS

MAINLAND

WALKWAYS

ISLETS

SPHERICAL

SKANSEN

STOCKHOLM

PARLIAMENT

GLASSBLOWING

ARCHIPELAGO

CANAL

MEDIEVAL

GREAT CHURCH

KULTURHUSET

GLOBEN

SWEDEN

WINDMILL

BRIDGES

Venice, Italy

In A.D. 400, settlers came from the Italian **mainland** to Venice. They established a trading community with Constantinople (now Istanbul, Turkey), the Italian mainland, and northern Africa. Venice soon developed into a beautiful community built floating in the sea. The houses, churches, and shops have to be supported by large posts driven deep into the mud. Today, the sea still threatens to swallow up Venice. Italian **engineers** and Dutch experts have created a successful system of water barriers and pumps to **stabilize** the sinking structures.

A **lagoon** separates Venice from the Italian mainland. Visitors must take a **ferry** across the Grand Canal to the city. There are no cars, buses, or trucks in Venice—only foot and boat traffic. Canals take the place of streets. All supplies are delivered to homes and businesses by boat. Some people live on houseboats in the canals because there is a shortage of reasonably- priced apartments. Gondolas, the traditional Venetian boats that are long and narrow, are **navigated** by gondoliers who use long poles to push off the bottom of the canal.

Saint Mark's Square is the city center. The Basilica of St. Mark, the **patron** saint of Venice, and the Doge's Palace are on the square facing the Grand Canal. The sidewalks are lined with cafes and shops for tourists. Priceless art treasures are displayed in the many churches of the city, but are locked tight for fear of theft. The only way to see many of the treasures is to visit during church services. There are also some amazing collections of paintings and sculptures in Venice's many museums and galleries that can be viewed.

Answer in complete sentences:

1. Where is Venice?
2. Why are parts of the city sinking?
3. What is a gondola?
4. What buildings are located in the city center?
5. When was the island first settled?

Web Sites:
http://www.virtualvenice.net/en
http://www.venetia.it/

Science

You will need:
- ✔ encyclopedia volume V
- ✔ paper
- ✔ pencil

The quality of life in Venice is threatened by air and water pollution. What effects has pollution had on the buildings and monuments of Venice? What has the Italian government done to help solve this problem?

Research

You will need:
- ✔ biography of Marco Polo
- ✔ paper
- ✔ pencil

Who is Marco Polo? What is his contribution to the history of Venice? List five important events from his life.

Art

You will need:
- ✔ prints by Italian artists
- ✔ paper
- ✔ pencil

Look at prints of work by Venetian artists Titian, Tintoretto, and Veronese. Choose one painting to describe. Name three other Italian painters or sculptors whose work may be displayed in a Venetian gallery.

Geography

You will need:
- ✔ detailed map of Italy and the islands of the Mediterranean
- ✔ drawing paper
- ✔ pencil

Draw a map of the Venetian Empire, showing Crete, Cyprus, and the Dalmatian Coast. Label Marghera and Mestre.

Daily Life in a Canal City

Consider a person's needs for food, shelter, clothing, transportation, employment, and entertainment. Explain how your life would be different as a citizen of Venice.

Complete the chart.

	Venice	My Town
Food		
Shelter		
Clothing		
Transportation		
Employment		
Entertainment		

Vienna, Austria

The city of Vienna is in northeastern Austria, **nestled** between the Alps and the Carpathian mountain ranges along the beautiful Danube River. This **eloquent** city, in such a scenic location, is a place of rich cultural background. The city has dark **baroque** architecture and a deep history. What began as a small Celtic trading village grew into a grand city famous for music, literature, and art.

Many of the most historic buildings and important landmarks are in the Inner City of Vienna, including Saint Stephen's Cathedral and the Hofburg Palace, home of Austria's president. The palace is a walled-in **compound** of many buildings. Beyond the Inner City is the *Ringstrassen*. Buildings in the *Ringstrassen* were built in the 1800s and include the **legendary** Opera House, Parliament, and the Stock Exchange.

Vienna is well known for its museums, libraries, and art galleries. Music is a very important part of Viennese life. All school children in Austria are required to learn a musical instrument. Vienna has raised some the world's finest classical **composers**, including Wolfgang Mozart, Franz Joseph Haydn, and Johann Strauss. Viennese concert halls regularly offer **opera**, instrumental, and ballet performances. The world famous Vienna Boys' Choir performs every Sunday at the Hofburgkapelle, one of the city's churches.

The Prater, a large amusement park, was first opened to the public in 1766. Once a private hunting ground for the king, the Prater now has something for all ages. It has a giant Ferris wheel, carousel, and a 2.5-mile (4-km) long miniature train. A planetarium and museum are also part of the park complex.

Answer in complete sentences:

1. Who were the first settlers of Vienna?
2. Who is Wolfgang Mozart?
3. What attractions are available at the Prater?
4. Where does Austria's president live?
5. What river runs through Vienna?

Web Site:
http://www.city.net/countries/austria/vienna

Research

You will need:
- ➤ nonfiction information about Vienna
- ➤ tour books
- ➤ Internet access (optional)
- ➤ paper
- ➤ pencil

Research information about the Vienna State Opera House. When was the building completed? Describe the interior of the hall. What opera was performed at the opening of the building?

Language Arts

You will need:
- ➤ German/English dictionary
- ➤ international cookbooks

Write a menu in the German language for one meal of traditional Austrian foods.

Music

You will need:
- ➤ music dictionary
- ➤ index cards
- ➤ markers

Make a matching game of 10 to 15 words and definitions (or symbols) relating to music. Play the game with a friend. Leave the game in the center for others to enjoy.

Music

You will need:
- ➤ nonfiction information about music history
- ➤ recordings
- ➤ paper
- ➤ pencil

Make a chart listing five compositions by each of these composers: Wolfgang Amadeus Mozart, Joseph Haydn, Franz Schubert, and Gustav Mahler. If possible, listen to some of each composer's music. Which one do you prefer? Explain.

Vienna, Austria

Use reference books to write a brief history of one of the attractions listed below. Indicate its exact address.

- Spanish Riding School
- The Prater
- State Opera House

- Schonbrunn Palace
- St. Stephen's Cathedral
- Hofburg Palace

Attraction _____

Address _____

_____

_____

_____

_____

_____

_____

_____

Draw three souvenirs that might be sold there.

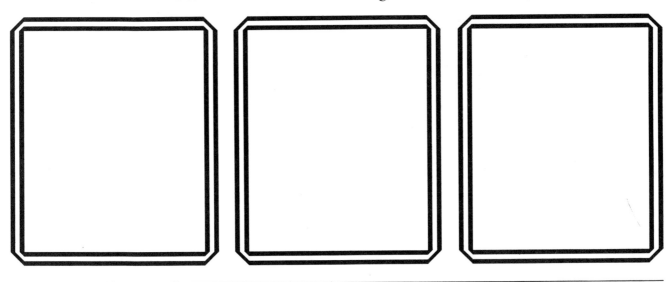

North and South America

North America is the third largest continent in the world. It includes Canada, Greenland, the United States, Mexico, Central America, and the islands of the Caribbean Sea. The main language spoken in Canada, the United States, and many Caribbean Islands is English. The main language in Mexico and Central America is Spanish.

About 458 million people live in North America. The earliest people, Inuits, crossed the Bering Strait to North America following animals to hunt. In the 1500s, British, French, and Spanish explorers established colonies in the United States and Canada. African slaves were first brought to the Caribbean by the Spanish to work on sugar plantations. Most North Americans have ancestors who have immigrated from Europe, Asia, or Africa.

The temperatures of North America range from bitter cold in the Arctic to steamy hot in the tropics. Greenland is permanently covered by ice. In the treeless North American tundra, the temperature is seldom above freezing. Most of North America has mild to cold winters and warm to hot summers with moderate amounts of rain and snow.

South America is the fourth largest continent in the world. The equator crosses South America through Brazil, Columbia, and Ecuador. It is almost totally surrounded by water. A narrow strip of land called the Isthmus of Panama connects Central America with Columbia.

South America has almost every kind of climate and landscape. The world's largest rain forest, the Amazon Basin, covers two-fifths of the continent. There are also deserts, grasslands, mountains, and active volcanoes. It is an area of great natural beauty, with spectacular waterfalls, snow-covered mountain peaks, and varied plant and animal life.

There are 12 independent countries in South America. Because of the mountains, rain forests, and deserts, most of the major cities are located near the coast. The main language spoken in South America is Spanish.

Bogota, Colombia

Bogota is a **lofty** city, **nestled** in the mountains about 8,600 feet (2,621 m) above sea level. The height provides the city with a comfortable cool climate, but can give visitors altitude sickness. This causes dizziness for a couple of days, until one's body **adjusts** to the thin air. The city crawls up the surrounding mountains, making it a scenic and **expansive** place.

All of Bogota can be seen in one breathtaking view from Monserrate, the area's tallest peak. This mountaintop can be easily identified by the church that crowns it. There is also a statue of the Fallen Christ that has become a **mecca** to Christians in the area. One gets to the holy place by a cable car that **precariously scales** the mountain. There are foot paths, but tourists are warned that they will surely be robbed by bandits hiding out in the jungle along the way.

Bogota is a city with a history dating back long before the Spanish came to Colombia. The first inhabitants were the Muisca, who formed a wealthy civilization. Their artwork, including pottery, **ceramics**, textiles, and gold artifacts, can be viewed at some of the city's best museums. The most interesting is the Gold Museum which has a collection of 30,000 golden treasures, most of which are held on the top floor in a huge **strongroom**. This amazing sight tells the story of an ancient society built out of gold.

Bogota is full of **contrasts**. The richest of the rich and the poorest of the poor share the crowded, traffic-jammed streets. There are towering skyscrapers built next to **dilapidated** shacks. The city is full of hothouse flowers grown for export to the United States. But there are also more dangerous exports shipped out of the city, such as cocaine. Bogota is a beautiful, but in some ways, a dangerous city.

Answer in complete sentences:

1. How does Bogota's altitude affect the weather?
2. Who are the Muisca?
3. What is at the top of Monserrate?
4 Where in Colombia is Bogota?
5. What is altitude sickness and what causes it?

Web Site:
http://lcweb2.loc.gov/frd/cs/cotoc.html

Research

You will need:

- ✔ travel brochures from Bogota
- ✔ travel agency number
- ✔ telephone access
- ✔ paper
- ✔ pencil

What is the cost of accommodations at the Bogota Hilton?
What is the address of the hotel?

Language Arts

You will need:

- ✔ nonfiction information about Bogota and Colombia
- ✔ paper
- ✔ pencil

Explain how rapid population growth has caused the creation of *barrios* in Bogota.

Art

You will need:

- ✔ nonfiction books about Bogota
- ✔ paper
- ✔ pencil
- ✔ art supplies

Make a book that shows different cultural activities and forms of entertainment enjoyed by the people of Bogota.

Music

You will need:

- ✔ nonfiction information about Spanish or South American music and traditional instruments
- ✔ paper
- ✔ pencil

Draw pictures and write a brief description of these instruments: bandola, maracas, and tiple.

Bogota, Colombia

Label the signs in this street scene.

church: la iglesia
meat market: el carnicería
restaurant: el restaurante
bicycle shop: la tienda de bicicleta
shoe repair shop: la zapatería

school: la escuela
market: el mercado
bakery: la panadería
police station: el estación de policía
barber shop: la barbería

Buenos Aires, Argentina

Buenos Aires is located on a bay called Rio de la Plata. City dwellers are called *portenos,* or people of the port. This is a **cosmopolitan** city which, it seems, identifies more with Europe than with the rest of **vast** Argentina. Sidewalk cafes, all-night bookstores, and numerous theaters, opera houses, and museums make up this **intellectual** city. Buenos Aires's modern, international atmosphere is a far cry from the small villages and pampas fields that fill Argentina.

The formal, civilized manners of *portenos* are **apparent** in Buenos Aires's parks. Until recently, it was against the law to wear shorts in the parks. Although not illegal, eating in the parks is highly frowned upon. It is common in the city to see very well-dressed ladies and gentlemen, seated on the park benches and quietly **chatting** or playing chess.

The restaurants in Buenos Aires are plentiful and serve many European-style pastas, cheeses, and wines. However, one distinctly Argentine flavor is the beef. Argentines have a huge vocabulary that identifies many different beef cuts and preparations. A typical meal begins with an **appetizer** of *chorizo,* a spicy pork sausage, or *morcilla,* blood sausage, before the main beef course is served. In between meals, cafes are filled with *portenos* drinking strong coffee and enjoying *dulce de leche,* a buttery caramel sauce, which is also served on toast in the morning.

Answer in complete sentences:

1. On what bay is Buenos Aires located?
2. What activities might one do in Buenos Aires's parks?
3. How are Argentina's city dwellers different from people in the small towns?
4. Who are the *portenos?*
5. What is *chorizo?* What is *dulce de leche?*

Web Site:

http://www.wam.com.ar/tourism/g/reg6/reg6.htm

Research

You will need:
- ✓ nonfiction books about professional athletes, soccer, and tennis
- ✓ paper
- ✓ pencil

Write a brief biography of Diego Maradona or Gabriela Sabatini.

Social Studies

You will need:
- ✓ atlas
- ✓ nonfiction books about Argentina
- ✓ paper
- ✓ pencil

Locate the Falkland Islands on a map. Explain who originally had control of the islands, and when and why, Argentina seized them.

Language Arts

You will need:
- ✓ nonfiction information about Argentina and Juan Peron
- ✓ paper
- ✓ pencil

Explain the popularity of Juan and Eva Peron. Who were their supporters? Who was their opposition?

Art

You will need:
- ✓ nonfiction books about South African costumes
- ✓ paper
- ✓ colored pencils

Make a drawing of a traditional gaucho costume.

Buenos Aires, Argentina

Use reference books or an encyclopedia to answer the following questions about Argentine independence.

1. In what year did the British invaders take over Buenos Aires?

   _____

2. How did the *portenos* feel about the British presence in their city? What did they do?

   _____

   _____

   _____

3. Where (in Buenos Aires) did the revolution take place?

   _____

   _____

   _____

4. What is the significance of May 25 to the Argentine people?

   _____

   _____

   _____

5. Who was José de San Martin? How did he help organize the Argentine independence movement?

   _____

   _____

   _____

6. What problems did independence cause in Argentina?

   _____

   _____

   _____

7. In what year was the democratic constitution adopted in Argentina?

   _____

   _____

   _____

Havana, Cuba

The capital of Cuba lies about 100 miles (161 km) south of Key West, Florida. The city stretches out along a beautiful coastline with palm trees and sandy shores. The Malecon is Havana's most famous **boardwalk**. The wide boulevard is lined with pastel-painted, colonial-style buildings that are faded and worn from sea air—just enough to give the area a **nostalgic** feel. Ocean waves crash against the rocks. Mist sprays the passersby. The city has very few skyscrapers.

The rest of Havana is a very well-preserved colonial town, one of the few that have remained untouched through the centuries.

Fidel Castro and a small group of **guerillas** overthrew the corrupt government of Fulgencio Batista in 1956. Castro wanted Cuba to be a socialist country. All foreign-owned property was nationalized and United States investors left Cuba. This has made getting certain necessities very difficult. Sometimes the Cuban people must line up at grocery stores to get what little supplies they can, like bread and flour. Gasoline is scarce in Cuba, so most cars are parked, waiting for **precious** fuel. This **inconvenience** has reduced traffic noise and air pollution, as only a limited number of buses and taxis fill the streets. Most Cubans have taken to riding bicycles for regular transportation.

The music in Havana reflects the spirited excitement of its people in spite of their economic difficulties. Cubans are mostly *mestizo* which is of mixed origin, generally African, Spanish, and **indigenous** ancestry. Their music reflects this rich mixture. Rumba refers to a kind of music, dance, and celebration. This style is thought to have originated during the **abolition** of slavery in Cuba. It is characterized by conga drums and lively beats. Mambo and jazz are also popular in the tropicana clubs in Havana. The famous *cha, cha, cha* craze began in Cuba. When it is combined with rumba, mambo, and jazz, it creates what is called salsa music.

Answer in complete sentences:

1. How far is Cuba from the United States?
2. Who is the prime minister of Cuba?
3. What is *mestizo?*
4. What is the Malecon?
5. On what date did Fidel Castro and his followers overthrow the government of Fulgencio Batista?

Web Sites:

http://www.lonelyplanet.com/dest/car/hav.htm
http://www.tomco.net/~larak/cuba/testcol.htm

Research

You will need:
- ✔ nonfiction information about Cuba
- ✔ paper
- ✔ pencil

What was life like for the people of Cuba under the government of Fulgencio Batista?

Language Arts

You will need:
- ✔ encyclopedia volume H
- ✔ paper
- ✔ pencil

Ernest Hemingway lived in a villa near Havana. Who was he? How is he remembered in Cuba?

Social Studies

You will need:
- ✔ encyclopedia volume H
- ✔ paper
- ✔ pencil

Havana has had a serious housing shortage since the 1960s. How has the government tried to solve the problem? Think about how other governments have addressed housing shortages and suggest two ways Cuba might improve living conditions for its people.

Art

You will need:
- ✔ nonfiction information about Cuba
- ✔ chart paper
- ✔ writing paper
- ✔ pencil

Explain how artists from all fields must justify their work in terms of Cuba's national interest. How are artistic and cultural activities influenced by the goals of the revolution? Head the chart paper Art, Music, and Literature. List the names of Cuban painters, composers, and writers or poets. Indicate some characteristics of nationalism in their work.

Havana, Cuba

Havana is the center of culture and art in Cuba. The country has a national symphony orchestra, ballet, and opera. Havana is the home of the National School of Fine Arts, National Ballet Institute, National Film Institute, and the Casa del Teatro (International Institute of Theater).

Posters have been a popular art form. Artists use them to communicate with the masses. A good poster uses few words and has a simple, but meaningful picture.

Design a poster to advertise a cultural event or movie in Havana. If you prefer, your poster may encourage the national interest in baseball or address a social issue like affordable housing, education, or health care.

La Paz, Bolivia

La Paz, is the largest city in Bolivia. At 12,000 feet (3,658 m) above sea level, it is the world's highest capital. The air is so thin at this height that the city never needed a fire department. (La Paz added one recently, just for show.) Fires cannot really **erupt** with such a little amount of **oxygen**. The center of the city lies in a deep, broad canyon formed by the Choqueyapu River. The snowcapped Andes Mountains overlook this breathtaking city and pockets of thick jungle surround it.

The Aymara, **descendants** of the ancient Inca civilization, live on the mountain slopes of La Paz. They make up about half of the city's population and still speak the old Uru or Puquina languages that were spoken even before the Incas existed. The Aymara live in small houses built from sun-dried mud bricks. Tin roofs are held down with large rocks. The women wear several brightly colored skirts at a time, called *polleras,* and blankets thrown over their shoulders with brown bowler-type hats. The men still farm the rocky mountain **terrain** as they have for centuries. The Aymara women sell colorful handmade **shawls** and blankets at open-air markets on the mountainsides.

Modern skyscrapers and government buildings are built further down the sides of the canyon. The Plaza Murillo is in the heart of the city. A huge modern cathedral and the Presidential Palace face the plaza. The government of Bolivia has been very unstable. It is in *The Guinness Book of World Records* as the country experiencing more **coups**, since 1825, than any other nation in the world.

Answer in complete sentences:

1. Name Bolivia's two capital cities.
2. Who were the Incas?
3. What mountain range overlooks La Paz?
4. Who lives on the mountain slopes?
5. What is a coup?

Web Sites:

http://travel.yahoo.com/destinations/South_America/Countries/Bolivia/Cities/La_Paz/
http://www.cs.purdue.edu/homes/krsul/bolivia/lapaz_intro.html

Research

Social Studies

You will need:
- ✔ paper
- ✔ pencil
- ✔ art supplies

Create a new product that the Aymara could sell in the markets of La Paz. Remember to use materials that are readily available to them. Make something that will be useful to many of the city people.

Research

You will need:
- ✔ map
- ✔ nonfiction books about Bolivia
- ✔ encyclopedia volumes L and S
- ✔ paper
- ✔ pencil

Explain why Bolivia has two capitals. What functions of government go on in each location? Compare the two cities and locate them on a map.

Art

You will need:
- ✔ nonfiction information about Bolivia
- ✔ pencil
- ✔ paper
- ✔ colored pencils or markers

The native people of Bolivia wear unique styles of head coverings. Read about three different culture groups. Make drawings of their hats and label each drawing with the name of the culture group.

Language Arts

You will need:
- ✔ nonfiction information about Bolivia
- ✔ pencil
- ✔ paper
- ✔ colored pencils or markers

Explain the Aymara festival of Alacitas. When is it held in La Paz? What is an *Ekeko?* Draw an *Ekeko* with at least five objects of personal importance to you.

La Paz, Bolivia

Help the Aymara woman find her way to market. Color the picture.

Mexico City, Mexico

Mexico City is the oldest continuously-inhabited city in the Western Hemisphere. The city is built on the site of the ancient Aztec city Tenochtitlán. It rests in a dry lake bed at the center of Mexico, halfway between the Gulf of Mexico and the Pacific Ocean, surrounded by mountains. The site of the city was chosen by an Aztec king when he had a vision of an eagle resting on a cactus. This was a sign from the Aztecs' powerful gods, so temples were built on that sacred location.

The *Zócalo*, or central **plaza**, of Mexico City, is where many museums, cathedrals, hotels, and government buildings are found. The National Palace, which **extends** for four square blocks, is the home of the country's executive offices. Inside the Palace are **murals** by the famous Mexican painter Diego Rivera depicting 500 years of Mexican history, including **idyllic** scenes of Aztec society before the Spanish invasion.

Nearby is Chapultepec Park, formerly the site of an Aztec market. The park includes a small zoo, **botanical** gardens, art and history museums, Chapultepec Castle, and the home of the president. Paseo de la Reforma passes directly through the park and was modeled after the Champs-Élysées in Paris, France. It is an eight-lane boulevard lined with shade trees and French-style mansions.

As the Reforma heads downtown, the mansions have been replaced with corporate headquarters, sleek office towers, and expensive hotels. Mexico City is still growing even though it is already the world's largest metropolis. The air pollution is so bad that walking outside for more than an hour can leave a film of dirt on your skin.

Answer in complete sentences:

1. Who were the Aztecs?
2. What is the Reforma?
3. What is Tenochtitlán?
4. What buildings are on the Zócalo?
5. What problems are caused by the congestion of people, cars, and industry in Mexico City?

Web Sites:

http://www.wotw.com/mexico/
http://mexico-travel.com/mexicocity/english/mex.html

Research

You will need:

➤ nonfiction information about Mexico City
➤ paper
➤ pencil

What problems does Mexico City have because of overpopulation? Compare and contrast Mexico City with your hometown.

Language Arts

You will need:

➤ paper
➤ pencil
➤ crayons or markers

Write and illustrate a two-page story about a day spent in Chapultepec Park.

Social Studies

You will need:

➤ nonfiction information about Mexico City
➤ travel brochures
➤ paper
➤ pencil

Plan a week-long trip to Mexico City with your family. Include travel costs and a packing list. What sights will you want to see?

Art

You will need:

➤ books about Mexican art and art history
➤ paper
➤ pencil

List the titles of three paintings or murals by Diego Rivera and three paintings by Frida Kahlo. Explain how these two famous artists were connected.

Mexico City, Mexico

Festivals, or *fiestas,* are held somewhere in Mexico almost every day of the year. They may last one or two days, or for as long as a week. Activities usually take place in the main plaza of the community.

The most important patriotic festival is Independence Day on September 16. It is celebrated in Mexico City with fireworks and the ringing of church bells. The president of Mexico appears on television to repeat the words of Father Miguel Hidalgo, who proclaimed Mexico's independence from Spain in 1810. The Zócalo, or central plaza, is filled with people.

The Day of the Dead is the most important religious festival of the year in Mexico. It blends European and Aztec beliefs about the spirit world and death. Special baked goods are made in the shape of coffins, skulls, and skeletons. They are offered to the returning souls of dead relatives. Families enjoy feasts and often keep a candlelight vigil at the local cemeteries.

Complete two of these activities:

▲ Do research to find the famous words of Father Miguel Hidalgo. Read them to the class.

▲ Make a drawing of the Column of Independence in Mexico City.

▲ Read more information about Mexican Independence Day. How is it like or unlike your own country's Independence Day?

▲ Read more information about the Mexican celebration of the Day of the Dead. How is it like or unlike the celebration of Halloween?

▲ Choose one other Spanish-speaking country. Explain how the people of that country observe the Day of the Dead.

▲ Make a drawing of a food table prepared for the Day of the Dead.

Montreal, Canada

Montreal is the second largest French-speaking city in the world after Paris, France. Located on an island in the St. Lawrence River, Montreal is the only city in North America that is built around a mountain. Mount Royal, from which the city takes its name, is a favorite spot for picnicking and various outdoor sports activities. The rest of Montreal is so flat that even though Mount Royal is not a particularly high mountain, it makes a lovely park from which to view the entire city.

About two-thirds of Montreal's residents are French Canadians. French is the official language. Street signs are in French and, in many schools, all instruction is in French. The government requires all **immigrants** to attend French language schools.

Old Montreal is on the waterfront. It is an area of **cobblestone** streets, historic churches, public squares, and fountains. Many of the buildings have been **restored** and now house modern cafes and **boutiques**. The city's oldest church, Notre-Dame-de-Bon-Secours, is in Old Montreal. The **stonework** on the front of the building is very simple, but the woodworking on the entrance and interior is very **ornate**. This was to **emphasize** the importance of Quebec's woodworking tradition.

Underground City is a special area of Montreal. It is the largest development of underground streets in the world with fine restaurants, stores, and movie theaters—a nice **retreat** when the winter weather is too harsh to walk the streets. Montreal's subway system, the Metro, is one of the best and quietest in the world. Its walls are decorated with brightly colored **mosaics** and each station has a **unique** design.

Answer in complete sentences:

1. What is the official language of Montreal?
2. What river runs through Montreal?
3. What is the capital of Quebec?
4. What is Underground City?
5. Where in Quebec is Montreal located?

Web Sites:

http://www.yahoo.com/Regional/Countries/Canada/Cities
http://www.cam.org/~fishon1/montrea.html

Research

You will need:
- ✔ nonfiction information about Montreal
- ✔ paper
- ✔ pencil

If you were opening a business in Montreal, what might be a good thing to sell? Explain your answer.

Language Arts

You will need:
- ✔ French/English dictionary
- ✔ paper
- ✔ pencil

Write in French: a list of 10 items you would pack for a trip to Montreal; a list of 10 foods you might find on a menu in Montreal; a greeting.

History

You will need:
- ✔ biography of Jacques Cartier
- ✔ encyclopedia volume C
- ✔ map of Canada
- ✔ paper
- ✔ pencil

Research Jacques Cartier's explorations in Canada. What waterways did he travel? Write one page describing his journeys.

Art

You will need:
- ✔ books on art history
- ✔ paper
- ✔ pencil

List three different works by Canadian artists that might be exhibited in the Montreal Museum of Fine Arts.

Underground City

Montreal's Underground City provides people with a convenient way to get around the city without having to deal with the weather. In winter or summer, visitors can stay dry and comfortable.

In the 1960s, several downtown office buildings, including Montreal's first skyscraper, Place Ville-Marie; the Place des Arts, a major cultural center; and the Metro subway system were constructed. The Underground City is a collection of subway stations, shopping malls, restaurants, hotels, theaters, high-rise apartments, and office towers, all connected by a network of underground tunnels. It is the largest development of its kind in the world.

It is possible to leave a downtown apartment in the morning, travel to work on the subway, go shopping, eat dinner, attend the theater, and return home without ever going outside.

The Metro is a rapid mass transit subway system connecting all the city's major attractions. Modern blue trains glide quietly beneath Montreal on rubber wheels. The 65 stations were designed by different artists and architects, creating a bold and colorful underground gallery.

Draw a picture of an underground city. Be sure to include at least three subway stations, two restaurants, an apartment building, a shopping mall with your favorite store, and a bakery.

New York City, United States

New York City is the largest city in the United States. Nicknamed the Big Apple, New York was the first capital of the United States, before Washington D.C. The world-renowned New York skyline is marked by the art deco Empire State Building and the glassy World Trade Center's twin towers. Block after block of towering skyscrapers, New York is truly a concrete jungle.

New York City is made up of five **boroughs**: the Bronx (on the mainland), Queens and Brooklyn (on Long Island), Manhattan, and Staten Island. Liberty and Ellis Islands make up the Statue of Liberty National Monument. Randall's Island has a sports and entertainment center and recreation areas. Riker's Island houses the city's prison **facilities**. Chinatown, Little Italy, Harlem, Soho, Wall Street, all within Manhattan, are some of the unique individual neighborhoods of this one big city.

New York City is an arts and entertainment **mecca**. Thousands of **aspiring** actors, artists, writers, and musicians **flock** to New York in hopes of "making it big." Besides hundreds of small art galleries, theaters, and night clubs where performers can get a start, New York has many famous cultural **venues** where major stars perform. Lincoln Center for the Performing Arts and Carnegie Hall have world-famous stages for opera, ballet, and orchestral concerts. Collections of fine art can be seen at the Metropolitan Museum of Art and the Guggenheim Museum. Broadway is the main place for the best in theater and musicals in the country.

Central Park in Manhattan was the first planned public park in the United States. This **haven** of green in the middle of the city has a small zoo, merry-go-round, and concert stage within its 840 acres.

Answer in complete sentences:

1. Name the five boroughs of New York City.
2. Where is the Statue of Liberty National Monument located?
3. What kinds of people are sent to Riker's Island?
4. Name three New York City landmarks.
5. How large is Central Park?

Web Sites:

http://nyctourist.com
http://city.net/united_states/new_york/new_york/

Research

You will need:
- ✔ nonfiction information about television studios and programs
- ✔ paper
- ✔ pencil

Make a list of 10 television shows that are produced in New York City. Indicate the company that produces each show.

Language Arts

You will need:
- ✔ nonfiction information about New York City
- ✔ paper
- ✔ pencil

Write a paragraph about life in one of New York City's boroughs.

Social Studies

You will need:
- ✔ tourist brochures about the Statue of Liberty National Monument
- ✔ paper
- ✔ pencil

Describe the Statue of Liberty National Monument. Explain its original connection to immigrants. What hours is it open to tourists? Is there an entry fee?

Art

You will need:
- ✔ resource book for the Metropolitan Museum of Art
- ✔ paper
- ✔ pencil

Make a list of 10 paintings or sculptures that are exhibited at the Metropolitan Museum of Art.

Empire State Building

The Empire State Building has 102 stories and stands 1,250 feet (381 m) high. Its architect, William Lamb, planned the offices around a center core of elevators, plumbing, and stairways. Work on the building was organized and precise. Some of the parts were built in factories and shipped to the building site. Limestone walls cover a steel frame that sways slightly in a strong wind. It took about a year to complete the building which was opened in 1931.

Today, the Empire State Building is the home to many small businesses. It is an important New York landmark. Tourists enjoy the view from the observation deck of the building where, on a clear day, they can see as far as New Jersey, Pennsylvania, Connecticut, and Massachusetts. The building recently celebrated its 65th birthday. It has been the location for more than 150 movies.

Choose one to complete:

▲ Research information about the life of William Lamb, the architect of the Empire State Building. Write a one-page biography on him.

▲ Research and explain what must be considered before beginning to build a skyscraper. Name at least two other skyscrapers in New York City.

▲ What do you imagine you would see on a clear day from the observation deck of the Empire State Building? Write a story describing the view and naming at least three specific locations.

▲ Name one movie that was shot from the observation deck of the Empire State Building. What makes the building a good setting for a movie?

Panama City, Panama

The Republic of Panama forms a **link** between Central and South America. The Atlantic and Pacific Oceans are connected by the Panama Canal which was opened in 1914. Panama City lies at the Pacific Ocean end of the Panama Canal. The canal is an amazing **engineering achievement** of the United States Army Corps of Engineers. The French attempted building it first in 1879, but after thousands of workers died in an accident, they gave up.

The original Panama City was a port village for trade and export. It was an open target for pirate raids because of its wealth. The English pirate Henry Morgan and his men burned and **plundered** the old city in 1671. The city was moved inland and walls were built around it for protection. Ruins of Panama La Vieja, or Old Panama, are preserved in a park outside modern Panama City. Within the walls is the Church of San Jose that houses a famous gold altar. This altar was painted black by a priest to hide it from the pirates.

Modern Panama City is full of skyscraper office buildings and hotels. Residents in the city live in high-rise condominiums. The busy streets are similar to any modern American city. Shops on Central Avenue sell locally- and foreign-made **goods**. These include jewelry, small electrical appliances, cameras, watches, and leather goods, which are sold at discount prices due to almost **duty-free** shipping.

Other attractions in Panama City include the large Convention Center overlooking the ocean, the Presidential Palace, the Museum of the Panamanian Man, and the Plaza de Francia. The Plaza de Francia (France Square) is the site of a monument to the French, honoring their involvement in the construction of the Panama Canal.

Answer in complete sentences:

1. What English pirate destroyed Panama City?
2. What can be purchased in the shops on Central Avenue?
3. When was the Panama Canal opened?
4. Where is the monument to the French who died building the Panama Canal?
5. How was the golden altar protected from pirates?

Web Site:

http://www.lonelyplanet.com/dest/cam/pan.htm

Research

You will need:

- ✔ map
- ✔ nonfiction information about the Panama Canal
- ✔ encyclopedia volume P
- ✔ paper
- ✔ pencil

Explain in detail the movement of a ship through the Panama Canal.

Language Arts

You will need:

- ✔ paper
- ✔ pencil

Is the Panama Canal important to the United States? What was the Panama Canal's main value when it opened in 1914?

Geography

You will need:

- ✔ map of the world
- ✔ drawing paper
- ✔ colored pencils

Draw a map of the Americas. Trace the route ships take passing through the Panama Canal from the Atlantic Ocean to the Pacific Ocean.

History

You will need:

- ✔ nonfiction information about Spanish explorers
- ✔ paper
- ✔ pencil

How did Vasco Balboa influence Panamanian history? How is he commemorated in Panama City?

Panama City, Panama

Word Search Puzzle

```
R E A P A C I F I C O C E A N O E B
I T X T H K P E N G K E O E A E E N
T A O A L E T A E A A S L H T O T I
E C E A C A S R N R O O T A V L M F
M A E G H N N S H A E T E D E E E E
L L F N N P A T R T M N N N G T E R
E I B A T N O V I A H A E N R N P E
E T D P E R E G N C G F I A G R R D
P A O N I S A R O R O R M N N A F U
U S E S O R I L O L E C I E U U D T
A G C T A O A M A E D P E Q M E O Y
Y O R A X N Y T N M P A S A R T T F
T H T O N R J I E I E E L E N S E R
T O D F N A G O H R C R D T E A O E
H R O E S N L S S N A N I I A I R E
O T H A E I O U A E U I R C E R T M
E P O R T R L R R L H P D L A C E P
S D A O A S F I P Y T D R S F P C D
```

Look for these words:

PANAMA

CENTRAL AMERICA

CANAL

PACIFIC OCEAN

ATLANTIC OCEAN

PORT

PIRATE RAIDS

HENRY MORGAN

GOLD ALTAR

DUTY-FREE

FRANCE SQUARE

SHIPPING

PRIEST

SAN JOSE

ENGINEERING

PLUNDERED

Reykjavik, Iceland

Reykjavik, on the southwest coast of Iceland, is the world's most northerly capital. The city was first settled by Ingolfur Arnarson, a Norwegian Viking. He named the city *Reykjavik*, meaning Bay of Smoke. This was actually steam, not smoke, rising from **hot springs** in the earth. Iceland is one the world's most **isolated** and **rugged** countries. Reykjavik depends almost entirely on imports, so it is an expensive place to live. However, it is one of the world's most civilized cities. There are no traffic jams and very little violence. The entire island's population is equal to the average amount of people in a United States suburb.

The old city center is where Ingolfur Arnarson first made his home. It is charming with parks, shops, and a Saturday **flea market.** Many of the buildings date back to the middle of the 18th century. The quiet Lake Tjorn makes a scenic backdrop for these simple buildings. Reykjavik is always **expanding.** The most **outstanding feature** of the modern skyline is a glass-domed, revolving restaurant called "the Pearl" that sits atop silvery hot-water tanks. The Laugardalur is the city's main green belt with an open-air, **geothermally-heated** swimming pool, soccer stadium, and an artificially-frozen skating rink.

Houses and apartments in Reykjavik are built of earthquake-proof concrete block. Many of them are painted in pastels with brightly colored roofs. All of the buildings are heated with water from hot springs 16 miles (25.7 km) away in Nesjavellir. Because of this, the city is very clean. There is little air pollution. There are no major industries on the island. The **staple** food, fish, are caught in the clean fresh waters of the nation's rivers and the ocean. The cattle and sheep in Iceland graze on land untouched by fertilizers or chemicals.

Answer in complete sentences:

1. Who was Ingolfur Arnarson?
2. Why is there little air pollution in Reykjavik?
3. What is the Laugardalur?
4. What is "the Pearl"?
5. Describe a typical home or apartment in Reykjavik.

Web Site:
http://www.lonelyplanet.comau/dest/eur/ice.htm

Research

You will need:

✔ encyclopedia volume H (hot springs) and E (energy supply)
✔ paper
✔ pencil

Explain how hot springs heat underground water for use as geothermal energy in the homes of Reykjavik.

Social Studies

You will need:

✔ paper
✔ pencil

The people of Iceland have a very long average life expectancy (men 75.8 years, women 80.2 years). Use what you know about an Icelander's way of life to explain this fact.

Science

You will need:

✔ nonfiction information about geysers, volcanoes, and glaciers
✔ paper
✔ pencil

Explain the effects of these natural phenomena (geysers, volcanoes, and glaciers) on the land and people of Iceland.

Science

You will need:

✔ nonfiction information about exotic birds
✔ paper
✔ pencil

Write a brief report on puffins. Explain their natural habitat in Iceland's bird cliffs.

Reykjavik, Iceland

You have been asked to explain to a nearby community the method that is used to heat the homes, public buildings, and water supply of Reykjavik.

Here are the facts:

▲ Hot springs form where surface water from rain and snow seeps into the ground and trickles through layers of hot molten rock.

▲ Power companies drill wells and pump hot water to the surface so that it can be used to generate energy.

▲ Reykjavik's District Heating System began in 1930 when water was piped to 70 homes, one school, and one swimming pool.

▲ The Reykjavik District System is the largest of its kind in the world, serving over half the population of Iceland.

▲ Geothermally-heated water is used for heating, washing, and bathing.

▲ Geothermally-heated water is also used in greenhouses that grow fruits and vegetables.

▲ There may be an odor of hydrogen sulphide in bath water.

▲ Reykjavik has less air pollution because it does not burn fossil fuels.

Make a list of advantages to using geothermal heat.

1. _____

2. _____

3. _____

4. _____

Are there any disadvantages?

_____

_____

_____

Rio de Janeiro, Brazil

Rio de Janeiro is called the *Cidade Maravilhosa* (Marvelous City) by Brazilians. Often called simply Rio, the city winds among the rugged shores of Guanabara Bay in the Atlantic Ocean. Sugar Loaf Mountain, one of the city's most famous landmarks, rises 1,325 feet (404 m) from a **peninsula** in the bay and can be visited by **cable car**. Rio is a favorite destination among tourists from around the world because of its white sand beaches, warm climate, and the spectacular Carnival celebration every year. **Amidst** the many hills of Rio, a huge statue called Christ the Redeemer stands on top of the highest hill, Corcovado. This magnificent monument keeps watch over a **thriving**, beachfront **metropolis**.

People who live in Rio are called *Cariocas*. Their **principle** language is Portugese. *Cariocas* are obsessed with soccer, which Brazilians call football. Maracaña Stadium, one of the largest arenas in the world, is in Rio. Brazil has won four out of the last nine World Cup football competitions (soccer). Brazil's national hero Pelé is recorded as the best player in history.

Rio comes alive with a wild celebration called Carnival which lasts for four days before **Lent**. The streets are filled with colorful, costumed dancers and bands playing **samba** music. All over the city and throughout Brazil, there are parades, dances, food, music, and contests. The most popular events during Rio's Carnival are the samba contests. The streets are blocked off and each of the 10 major samba schools in Rio marches while playing. Each band may have up to 3,000 dancers and supporters parading along behind it. The contest goes on through the night. There are also nonstop parties in the streets and in the elite private clubs of Rio.

Answer in complete sentences:

1. Explain the meaning of the terms *Cariocas* and *Cidade Maravilhosa*.
2. Who is Pele?
3. For what kind of music is Rio known?
4. In what bay is Rio located?
5. How is Carnival celebrated in Rio?

Web Site:
http://www.geocities.com/Heartland/Ranch/2012

Research

You will need:
- ✔ nonfiction information about soccer
- ✔ paper
- ✔ pencil

Explain the importance of soccer to Brazilian culture. Name Rio's two professional teams. List the country's World Cup victories.

Art

You will need:
- ✔ encyclopedia volume B (Brazil)
- ✔ paper
- ✔ pencil
- ✔ markers

What ethnic foods are most popular in Brazil's cities? What are *manioc, feijoada, churrasco,* and *batidas?* Design an illustrated menu showing these items.

Social Studies

You will need:
- ✔ map of South America
- . ✔ paper
- ✔ pencil

Draw the shape of South America. Outline the country of Brazil. Label Rio de Janeiro, São Paulo, Brasília, and all the bordering countries.

Music

You will need:
- ✔ nonfiction information about Carnival
- ✔ colored pencils or markers
- ✔ paper
- ✔ samba recording

Listen to a recording of samba music and design a Carnival parade float or poster.

Rio de Janeiro, Brazil

Use a map of Rio de Janeiro from an atlas or an encyclopedia. Read and follow the directions.

▲ Color the Christ the Redeemer (Corcovado) statue yellow.
▲ Color Lake Rodrigo de Fréitas blue.
▲ Color the mountain areas brown.
▲ Draw an umbrella on Ipanema Beach.
▲ Draw a surfer in the Atlantic Ocean at Copacabana Beach.
▲ Circle Sugar Loaf Mountain.
▲ Draw a sailboat in the Bay of Guanabara (Baia de Guanabara).
▲ Draw a soccer ball near Maracaña Stadium.
▲ Draw a flower near the Botanical Gardens.

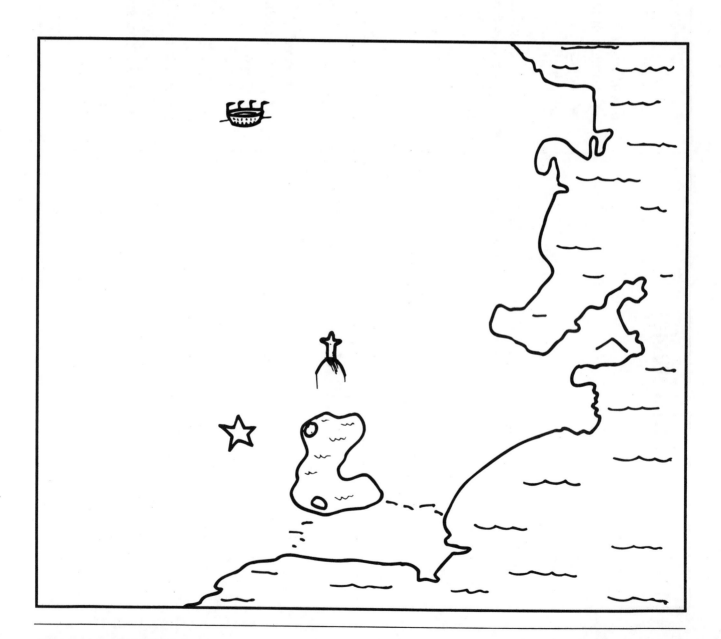

San Francisco, United States

San Francisco is located on a peninsula between the Pacific Ocean and San Francisco Bay in western California. The **strait** between the two bodies of water is called the Golden Gate. It is **spanned** by a famous **suspension bridge**. This bridge, the Golden Gate Bridge, is over 2 miles (3.2 km) long with towers that reach heights equal to a 48-story building. San Francisco was almost **levelled** in an earthquake and fire in 1906. The city was rebuilt and continues to **thrive**, even though earthquakes still threaten its existence.

San Francisco is built on hills like rollercoasters. An unusual means of public transportation and one of San Francisco's most popular tourist attractions are cable cars. These cars do not use engines or electricity. They run on **kinetic energy** that builds up in the steel cables. The inventor was said to have watched a horse-drawn cart slide helplessly down one of the city's steep hills, dragging the horses behind. This inspired the inventor to design the first cable car.

San Francisco has the largest Chinese community outside of Asia. Thousands of immigrants came to San Francisco in the 1860s to work on the railroad or as merchants hoping to make a fortune in America's gold **boomtown**. Chinatown is a **district** of colorful restaurants, temples, and shops that sell Chinese traditional herbs, foods, and crafts. Groups of people gather at dawn in some of the squares in Chinatown to perform *tai chi*, an ancient Chinese form of exercise and relaxation.

Fisherman's Wharf, located east of the Golden Gate Bridge, has a floating museum, seafood restaurants, and a busy fish market. Ghiradelli Square and The Cannery, former factories, have been made into multilevel shopping centers. Golden Gate Park is one of the largest **cultivated** parks in the country with over 1,000 acres of forests, streams, lakes, and waterfalls.

Answer in complete sentences:

1. Where is San Francisco located?
2. How long is the Golden Gate Bridge?
3. Why did many Chinese immigrants come to San Francisco?
4. Why are cable cars important in San Francisco?
5. What is *tai chi?*

Web Site:
http://www.backinsf.com/

Research

You will need
- ✔ encyclopedia volume S
- ✔ paper
- ✔ pencil

What products were made in Ghiradelli Square and The Cannery when they operated as factories? What was the original use for Alcatraz Island?

Research

You will need
- ✔ encyclopedia volume S and C (cable car)
- ✔ paper
- ✔ pencil

Briefly describe how a cable car works. Who invented them?

Science

You will need
- ✔ encyclopedia volume S
- ✔ paper
- ✔ pencil

Describe the events of the San Francisco earthquake on April 18, 1906? When was the city's next major earthquake? How has being in an earthquake-prone area influenced construction in the city? Sketch a map showing the San Andreas fault.

Social Studies

You will need:
- ✔ nonfiction information about the gold rush
- ✔ paper
- ✔ pencil

How was San Francisco affected by the discovery of gold at Sutter's Mill?

Chinatown, San Francisco

Chinatown is a unique neighborhood defined by the culture and traditions of its people. It is the largest Chinese community outside of Asia. The narrow streets are crowded and noisy. Older residents and immigrants live in small apartments above and behind businesses. Chinese-style buildings are decorated with brightly colored lanterns and calligraphy on sign boards. The Chinese language is heard in the restaurants, shops, and temples.

Many other cities have a Chinatown. Research one of these Chinatowns. Compare it to San Francisco's Chinatown.

_____

_____

_____

_____

_____

_____

_____

_____

_____

_____

_____

_____

_____

_____

_____

Toronto, Canada

Toronto, which means "the meeting place," was originally named by the Huron more than 400 years ago. Today, Toronto is the largest city in Canada. It lies on the shores of Lake Ontario, one of the smaller Great Lakes. This lake is still large enough to give Toronto the feel of an ocean port. Its beaches are popular in summer. The Toronto Islands are just offshore from the harbor for biking and picnicking.

Toronto is a fast-paced, **productive** city as the country's financial center. The CN (Canadian National) Tower, at 1,815 feet (553 m), is the world's tallest **freestanding** structure. The Eaton Centre houses Toronto's largest department store, Eaton's, 300 other stores, and 2 high-rise office buildings. Toronto's SkyDome is a modern sports stadium with the world's first **retractable** dome. This **enables** sports fans to enjoy the Blue Jays (Toronto's professional baseball team) in the fresh air or the Maple Leafs (Toronto's professional hockey team) in the **dead** of winter. The sports complex includes a hotel, restaurants, meeting rooms, and a health club.

Toronto has major symphony orchestra, opera, and ballet companies. The Royal Ontario Museum is the largest museum in Canada. There are more than 100 parks in the city, including the Toronto Zoo and Wonderland, an amusement park. High Park is the largest, offering rentable paddle boats, an outdoor theater, nature trails, and huge open spaces. The Hockey Hall of Fame is downtown and so is the City Hall complex, complete with its own ice skating rink.

Answer in complete sentences:

1. What does the word "Toronto" mean?
2. What buildings are in Toronto's Eaton Centre?
3. Why is the CN Tower a famous landmark?
4. What sports are represented by Toronto's professional teams?
5. On what lake is Toronto located?

Web Sites:

http://www.toronto.com
http://www.torontodirect.com

Geography

You will need:
- ✔ detailed map of Canada
- ✔ drawing paper
- ✔ pencil

Draw a map of Ontario, the Great Lakes, and St. Lawrence Seaway. Label Toronto and five other cities near the lakes.

Research

You will need:
- ✔ nonfiction books about Canada
- ✔ paper
- ✔ crayons or markers
- ✔ pencil

What are the dates for these Canadian holidays: Boxing Day, Canada Day, Thanksgiving Day, and Victoria Day? Choose one holiday to research further. How is it observed? Design a greeting card with an appropriate holiday verse.

Art

You will need:
- ✔ paper
- ✔ colored pencils
- ✔ markers

Design a logo and write an advertising slogan to attract business to Toronto's Eaton Centre.

Research

You will need:
- ✔ nonfiction information about hockey
- ✔ paper
- ✔ pencil

The Hockey Hall of Fame is in downtown Toronto. List the names of five players in the Hockey Hall of Fame.

Toronto, Canada

Toronto, Ontario, has four professional sports teams.

Use reference books to:
▲ Determine the win/loss records for the previous season of each team.
▲ Name two players from each of the teams.

	Toronto Bluejays	Toronto Argonauts	Toronto Maple Leafs	Toronto Raptors
Win/Loss Record				
Player				
Player				

Explain the rules for Canadian football. How does it differ from American football?

_____

_____

_____

_____

_____

_____

_____

_____

Answer Key

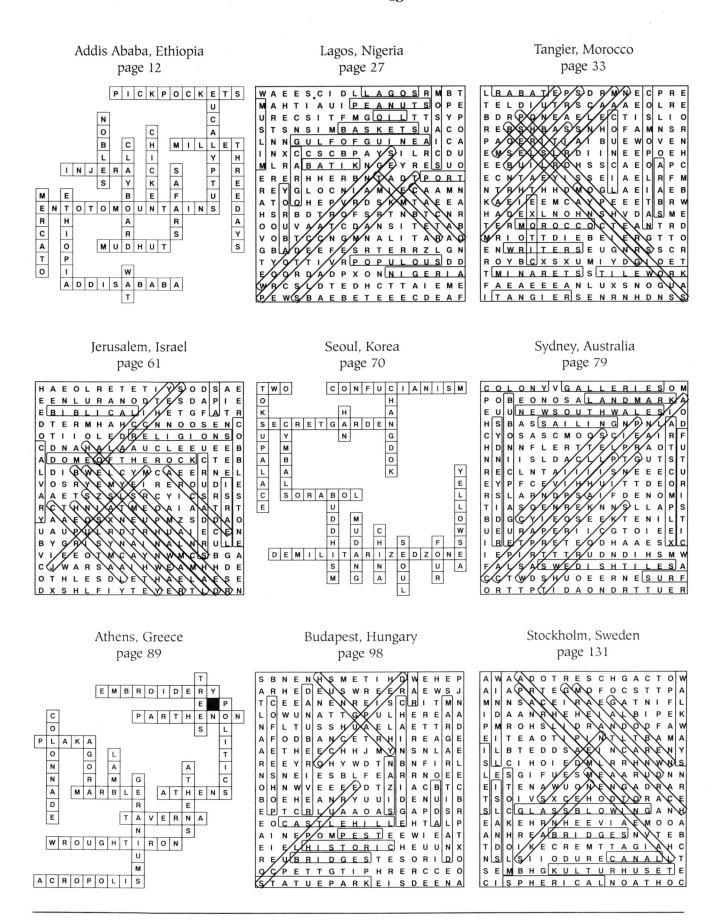

Addis Ababa, Ethiopia
page 12

Lagos, Nigeria
page 27

Tangier, Morocco
page 33

Jerusalem, Israel
page 61

Seoul, Korea
page 70

Sydney, Australia
page 79

Athens, Greece
page 89

Budapest, Hungary
page 98

Stockholm, Sweden
page 131

Panama City, Panama
page 162

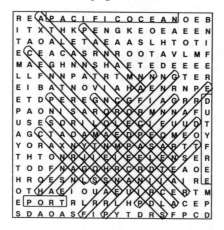

Reference List

Edwards, Mike. 1997. Hong Kong: Countdown to China. *National Geographic*. March, Vol. 191. No. 3. p. 32.

Ellis, William, S. 1994. Shanghai: Where China's Past and Future Meet. *National Geographic*. March, Vol. 185. No. 3. p. 2.

Mairson, Alan. 1996. The Three Faces of Jerusalem. *National Geographic*. April, Vol. 189. No. 4. p. 2.

McCarry, John. 1995. Bombay: India's Capital of Hope. *National Geographic*. March, Vol. 187. No. 3. p. 42.

Newcott, William, R. 1993. The Living Tower of London. *National Geographic*. October, Vol. 184. No. 4. p. 36.

Parfit, Michael. 1996. Mexico City: Pushing the Limits. *National Geographic*. August, Vol. 190. No. 2. p. 24.

Putnam, John, J. 1994. Buenos Aires: Making Up for Lost Time. *National Geographic*. December, Vol. 186. No. 6. p. 84.

Range, Peter Ross. 1996. Reinventing Berlin. *National Geographic*. December, Vol. 190. No. 6. p. 96.

Raymer, Steve. 1993. St. Petersburg: Capital of the Tsars. *National Geographic*. December, Vol. 184. No. 6. p. 96.

Reid, T. R. 1995. The Great Tokyo Fish Market: Tsukiji. *National Geographic*. November, Vol. 188. No. 5. p. 40.

Reid, T. R. 1997. The World According to Rome. *National Geographic*. August, Vol. 192. No. 2. p. 61.

Remnick, David. 1997. Moscow: The New Revolution. *National Geographic*. April, Vol. 191. No. 4. p. 78.

Roberts, David. 1995. Age of Pyramids: Egypt's Old Kingdom. *National Geographic*. January, Vol. 187. No. 1. p. 2.

Stanfield, James, L. 1989. The New, the Enduring Paris. *National Geographic*. July, Vol. 176. No. 1. p. 6.

Swerdlow, Joel, L. 1993. Central Park: the Oasis in the City. *National Geographic*. May, Vol. 183. No. 5. p. 2.

Theroux, Peter. 1993. Cairo—Clamorous Heart of Egypt. *National Geographic*. April, Vol. 183. No. 4. p. 38.

Zwingle, Erla. 1995. Venice: More Than a Dream. *National Geographic*. February, Vol. 187. No. 2. p. 70.